THE GREAT SACRIFICE

Studies in Hopkins

David Anthony Downes

UNIVERSITY
PRESS OF
AMERICA

LANHAM • NEW YORK • LONDON

PR
4803
H44
Z494
1983

Copyright © 1983 by
Tallahassee, Florida
University Press of America,™ Inc.

4720 Boston Way
Lanham, MD 20706

3 Henrietta Street
London WC2E 8LU England

Printed in the United States of America

Library of Congress Cataloging in Publication Data

Downes, David Anthony, 1927–
    The great sacrifice.

    1. Hopkins, Gerard Manley, 1844–1889--
Religion and ethics--Addresses, essays, lectures.
2. Poets, English--19th century--Biography--
Addresses, essays, lectures.
1. Title.
PR4803.H44Z494   1983   821'.8   [B]   83-3619
ISBN 0-8191-3142-3
ISBN 0-8191-3143-1 (pbk.)

This collection of essays is dedicated to the late John Pick and D. Anthony Bischoff, S.J., whose care for Hopkins has ever been an inspiration for me as a student, friend, and colleague--"Fonder a care kept than we could have kept it, kept/Far with fonder a care (and we, we should have lost it)...."

ACKNOWLEDGMENTS

I wish to thank the publisher of *Thought* for permission to reprint "The Hopkins Enigma" and the editor of *The Hopkins Quarterly*, Richard F. Giles, for his generosity in allowing me to reprint revised versions of "Beatific Landscapes in Hopkins" and "Grace and Beauty in 'The Wreck of the Deutschland': A Centenary Estimation." Also I much appreciate the support and interest of other Hopkins scholars and students such as John Pick, D.A. Bischoff, S.J., James Hall, Theodore Roethke, Robert Heilman, M.C. D'Arcy, S.J., Eugene R. August, Robert Boyle, S.J., Paul Mariani, Alan Heuser, Alison G. Sulloway, and Norman H. MacKenzie. Finally gratitude is here expressed to the Society of Jesus for the "fair use" of quotations from Hopkins' poetry and prose, to all authors and publishers whose work I have quoted and cited, and to Shirley M. Mills and Deborah Perkins for excellent assistance in preparing the typescript.

CONTENTS

PREFACE

In George Bernard Shaw's *St. Joan*, Captain Robert de Baudercourt asks of Saint Joan, "How do you mean? voices?" Joan answers, "I hear voices telling me what to do. They come from God." Robert tells her, "They come from your imagination." Joan replies: "Of course. That is how messages of God come to us."

The imagination in its high powers has ever been an instrument of "talking" to God. Whatever the hidden witness in religious experience, it has been the sanctifying imagination which has translated religious mystery into the spiritual imagery which constitutes the sacral consciousness.

This collection of essays represents a lengthy reflection upon the life and work of one of the great religious spirits among the "visionary company," Gerard Manley Hopkins. Two essays in this collection are given over to studying the mysteries of Hopkins' life. The first, written over thirty years ago and now updated, examines the enigmas that his story presents, and continues to present, even up to the latest biographical inquiries. The second biographical essay attempts to delineate what may have been a major pattern in his personal makeup, that of always seeking a counterpoise between the poet and priest in him through which these two, great, directory powers of his personality might creatively cooperate.

The last two essays are investigations of the spiritual landscapes of Hopkins' religious imagination. My first exploration of this subject was a study of the influences of St. Ignatius de Loyola upon Hopkins' poetry and imagination as a result of his becoming a Jesuit (*Gerard Manley Hopkins: A Study of His Ignatian Spirit*, Twayne, 1960). In this book I laid out the patterns of one of the most central, shaping forces of the Christian tradition which impacted Hopkins' work profoundly. This book was followed by another examination of a second, shaping force upon Hopkins, that of Walter H. Pater (*Victorian Portraits: Hopkins and Pater*, Twayne, 1965). In this book I attempted to uncover through close study of the minds and temperaments of Hopkins and Pater the implications which Romanticism had for the Christian, religious imagination. I found a new understanding of religious assent developing, largely and principally through the employment of the religious imagination as a translator of personal, religious experience.

ix

Romanticism in its high, visionary mode began in
the last century to authenticate images of God based
upon the imaginative assimilation of intense, personal,
religious experience. Out of this creative fusion of
esthetic encounter and affective assent came new expressive forms of religious consciousness, deeper structures
involving visionary transport and transcendence. To
test the validity and extent of this cultural insight, I
studied three Victorian authors whose writings, given
the relevance of their lives and work to this issue,
ought to be proving ground for validating such a significant change in human thought and experience. I
chose the most famous Protestant convert of the century
whose writings form a major part of the development of
religious thought of his time, John Henry Newman. The
second author, whose writings I analyzed, was a major
representative of that Victorian, religious hybrid, the
High Church fundamentalist, Charles Kingsley. The third
writer I examined, a representative of the religious
estheticism and agnosticism which became so significant
an element in English Romanticism in its later evolu-
tion, was Walter H. Pater. His thought could be use-
fully contrasted with that of Newman and Kingsley in
showing the direction of the theological imagination in
both its Christian and non-Christian aspects. While in
this book I surveyed much of their prose, I concen-
trated upon their attempts to employ the religious imagination to account for personal, religious experience,
the character of faith and personal assent. The book
thus focuses mainly on the religious novels of these
three authors (*The Temper of Victorian Belief: Studies
in the Religious Novels of Pater, Kingsley and Newman*,
Twayne, New York, 1972). I found the Victorian religious novel to be one of the developing forms of the
religious imagination through which a new understanding
of spirituality and faith was being expressed. Recently
I have added John Ruskin to this investigation of the
religious imagination because of his great passion for
and sensitivity to religious inconography (*Ruskin's
Landscape of Beatitude*, University Microfilms, International, 1980).

In these last essays, I have undertaken to explore
the religious motifs and images of Hopkins' religious
imagination. One essay is given over to seeing the pattern of common experience underlying Hopkins' great
ode, "The Wreck of the Deutschland." Here my critical
effort is to see how Hopkins' Christian, Romantic, religious imagination has transfigured human love into
divine love. A second essay lays out the general pattern of deific vision throughout Hopkins' major poetry,

surveys the spiritual topography of the beatific landscapes in his poetry, and discusses the unique character of his religious imagination. The focus is upon
the unusual sanctifying character of his use of the religious imagination as he tried to "inscape" the "great
sacrifice" of Christ in his own life and in his poetic
and priestly work. Reflections are offered for including Hopkins in the "visionary company" of the great,
high Romantics because the ways that God appeared in
his religious imagination have not been equaled since
John Donne.

THE HOPKINS ENIGMA

Among readers of G. M. Hopkins, two attitudes with
many variations prevail concerning the significance of
the man in his works. One view, which might be aptly
called the Religious, is that Hopkins was a near-saint
who expressed the glories of Christian spirituality with
a truly Christian disposition about their secular value.
In God's providence, his work has been preserved, published, and now takes its place among the rarer triumphs
of the Victorian Age.

The other view can be called New Critical: Hopkins
suffered from infirm health, an excessively acute conscience, deep guilt complexes, and a strong, intro-
punitive complex aggravated by Catholicism and the
priesthood. This caused him to suppress his artistic
powers, the dominant facet of his personality. The result was a lifetime of continuous psychological stress
abetted by a weakened physique. His personality patterns were mildly but increasingly psychoneurotic with
some depressive reaction tendencies. With the suppress-
ing of his artistic desires, his dominant personality
stabilizers, he suffered a gradual breakdown during his
last years, culminating in his death. A careful textual
reading of his papers and poems makes this clear, especially the last poems he wrote while he was in Dublin.

I am sure one of the foregoing paragraphs will of-
fend some readers not only because of the contrary alle-
giances in each, but also because the supporting data
are enigmatic: He, an artist, feared the artistic life;
he possessed a finely balanced objective moral sense yet
personally was intensely scrupulous; his writing is
filled with a dramatic sense of action and accomplishment though in his own life he found it hard to get anything done; he was, even as a religious, a truly holy
person, yet his feelings of guilt enervate his spirit;
possessing the stoutest confidence in his intellectual
commitments and his poetic achievements, he still was
unable to bring himself to ask for routine permissions
to publish as his friends urged; he lived and died in
obscurity although today he is ranked with the finest
poets of his time.

The negative and positive pattern of these facts is
more than circumstantial irony. They are the pieces of
tragedy and comedy. The focus of the tragedy in Hopkins' life is without doubt his inability to reconcile
his poetic personality with his vocation. From the time

it is first mentioned early in his letters, it keeps surfacing again and again, always with the greatest control. It was in his private notebooks and retreat jottings where the ferocity and terrible damage of his struggle are recorded. The "terrible sonnets" are more than statements of the plight of a man whose grand dedication has become barren; read in conjunction with the retreat notes written at the same time, they take on the enormous, suffering acquiescence of tragedy.

The focus of comedy in Hopkins' life is surely his great love of God. There is comedy that mocks and that which rejoices; the first kind can through Christian hope lead to the second. Mundane eyes often see only the first kind of which there is probably no unkinder cut than Hopkins' resorting to his poetry when trying to confront his overpowering spiritual status near the end of his life. Against besetting moments like these, and there were many, must be put Hopkins' immense poetic joy at discovering God in all things and his noble acceptance of the promises of Christ.

The Religious view tends to see the comedy and the New Critical the tragedy. Which is nearer the reality?

Recent biographical study suggests that the truth of the matter lies in fusing these two views. I should like to outline a third view which I shall call tragicomic. This view proposes a composite of Hopkins in which man, priest, and poet ally themselves in patterns of relationships which are deeply serious and of great magnitude--a personal tragedy, and yet which in another perspective represent an enormous personal victory. The emphasis, I would suppose, will depend on whether the biographer dwells on the sacrifices or the reasons for making them. However, no definitive biography can ignore these two dimensions of Hopkins' life.

But first we must examine the biographical vacuities in his genesis which obscure such important moments in his life.

No biographer has adequately presented Hopkins' family. His mother and father, for example, remain but instrumental causes in the first few pages of Chapter One. We are told that Gerard and his father had the same kind of minds: deep in fact, generic in conception, and artistic in expression. Manley's treatise on *The Cardinal Numbers* is usually cited in support. We are also told that it was his father who stimulated the arts in the family through his own interest in poetry, although it is possible that an aunt had greater influence, especially on Gerard. What we are not told about is his father's inability to give his son an appreciation of accomplishment except in the form of a middle name. Hopkins spent all his life trying to get something done as his notebooks and letters make so painfully clear.

It is possible that Manley Hopkins never asked much action of his son because of the latter's frailty. Gerard was small in stature, anemic in body. It is very likely that he remained the special charge of his mother. Biographers describe Kate Hopkins as "gentle" and inclined to "metaphysical speculation." The first attribute befits a mother, and she undoubtedly exercised it on Gerard. However, the second is hardly a leading trait of motherhood. One suspects that a mother given to such intellectual interests might very well incite her children to similar interests, but this is peripheral to our wonders about the affective relationships she established with a son who was frail, sensitive, and highly intelligent. It would seem that he needed little of the metaphysical and a good deal of the physical.

Any sound biography will have to probe Hopkins' relationships with his parents for evidence to explain his own fear of his passions, his scrupulous conscience, his obsession with regular penances often of a physical nature, his stubborn tendency to set arbitrarily hard goals for himself and then berate himself into accomplishing them, his general blindness to ordinary human life for which was substituted the eagle's eye of the naturalist. Perhaps here lies an explanation for a definite lack of masculinity in Hopkins, which no biographer can afford to overlook, and while this attribute may have enhanced his artistic sensibility by providing it with a special delicateness, it may have been a powerful causative factor in much of his failure in his mature life. It has been pointed out that his writing is filled with deeds, feats of action glowing in his verbal admiration. Against this must be set the biographical fact that his main doing was giving it all up.

It is possible that this trait of manly capability has something positive to do with his spiritual courage, for it is true that while as a teen-ager he was cultivating music and painting with promising success, he was also developing a personal moral code so high in its

3

demands that it emphasized pride more than virtue and promised agony in the face of inveterate human frailty. He seems to have demanded perfections of himself that he could accept psychologically as superior to any typically masculine endeavors, few of which really attracted him. These can be seen as defenses against really being effeminate.

The impression he made at Highgate clearly indicates the dominant pattern of his personality and character. He excelled in his command of language (he won two prizes for his poetry) which showed that his forte was in poetry. Coupled with his artistic nature was his moral code. He had a reputation for absolute truthfulness and his powers of perseverance. When a high-school boy excels in morality, he warrants his headmaster's careful scrutiny, for such character is often not the sign of moral health, but rather the symptom of personality decompensation. Moreover, a poet is a seer of life, but if he has scruples about looking, as Hopkins told Mowbray Baillie, he is bound to be cast into a quandary. This, unfortunately, is just what happened to Hopkins. Through the Highgate years, these two opposites in him seem to have lain in peaceful coexistence, but war between the poet and conscience (ultimately his vocation) began in the Oxford years, a kind of microcosm of the Victorian dilemma.

To any biographer, the university years are very important ones because they represent generally their subject's coming of age. It is at this time that the first signs of maturity manifest their telltale directions. This is certainly so for Hopkins, for these years reveal in clear contrast the artist and the ascetic in him. He made choices at this time which set him on a course of life during which these two deep and abiding forces were to collide painfully between periods of delicate reconciliation. This was the only time in his life that he was really in rapport with his age. After this, he found himself an alien, to Britain and to this world. It made him sad, but it was true.

In 1863, when Hopkins went up to Balliol, almost twenty years after Newman had become a convert to Catholicism, Oxford still harbored some of those whose unabashed devotion to Christianity and the Anglican Church could not be diminished by the Roman ruse that publicly thwarted the Movement. By now, of course, their influence was largely upon the students to whom they quietly gave their lights amidst a waxing of

4

skepticism all around them. Hopkins was one of those whose religious practice was invigorated along Anglo-Catholic lines as his diaries attest with their scrupulous recording of misdemeanors, failings, and sins that he deleted as he confessed them to Dr. E. B. Pusey. But it was not High Church leaders such as Pusey or H. P. Liddon who, despite their frequent contact with young Hopkins in academic and religious matters, had a stamping influence on him, but rather the spirit of Newman, whom, undoubtedly, every High Churchman was bound to explain to all who received their calls.

When we consider the intellectuality of those philosophical essays which Hopkins wrote for his mentors (one of whom was Walter Pater whose esthetical attitudes are often in agreement with Hopkins' despite deep, ethical differences), it is not surprising that the dilemma which Newman faced was understood by the youthful Hopkins. He could have easily been concerned, had he been shallow, with the modes of religious ritual, forms of church architecture, traditions of sacred music, and not with the logical implications behind them. Perhaps nothing is more suggestive of the failure of the Oxford Movement than its concern, in the years after its public rejection, with the secondary elements of Christianity which, in their Italian and French forms, were so alien to English devotional habits. Newman told Pusey as much in 1865.[1] But Hopkins, like Newman, was soon brought to the overwhelmingly personal issue of the English religious question. I put this down to his intellectual integrity, a rare quality which sometimes hurt him with some of his fellow members of the Society of Jesus. In his Platonic dialogue, *On the Origin of Beauty*, for example (possibly written for Pater), there is apparent in the youthful Hopkins a driving quality to get at the truth by searching inquiry and hard reason. He was later to call this attitude a "being in earnest with...reality,"[2] a point of view which he deemed essential to all significant art. Such a mind possessed a seriousness that could not see the question of the Apostolic origin of the Anglican Church as merely academic. For him, Newman's deeply pondered questions, "Can I (it is personal, not whether another, but can I) be saved in the English Church? Is it mortal sin in *me*, not joining another communion,"[3] were primary before all the other besetting doubts. Great conflicts not only define universal issues; they also define men. Whatever answers he finally chose, here was a quality of religious faith that can only be admired for its chasteness and commitment. Even those who discount religion would find few among their fellows so totally dedicated to skepticism. Total sincerity is a rarity in the shape of any personal life, and no biographer can fail to describe its abiding power in Hopkins. It is really at the basis of all his failures and successes. It is what Coventry Patmore meant when he wrote to Bridges six years after Hopkins' death: "Gerard Hopkins was the only orthodox, and as far as I could see, saintly man in whom religion had absolutely no narrowing effect upon his general opinions and sympathies."[4] These were the impressions of a man who was with Hopkins face to face but eight days of his life and received twenty-six letters from him. Nevertheless, the impression was a deep one, so compelling that Patmore told Bridges, "The *authority* of his goodness was so great with me that I threw the manuscript of a little book—a sort of 'Religio Poetae'—into the fire, simply because, when he read it, he said with a grave look, 'That's telling secrets.' This little book had been the work of ten years continual meditations, and could not have but made a greater effect than all the rest I have ever written; but his doubt was final with me."[5]

Hopkins' preoccupation with religion during his Oxford days is nowhere more revealed than in his intermittent verse writing. In that section of Gardner's edition entitled "Early Poems" there is not a poem that does not reveal an ascetic attitude, and most are explicitly religious. Even though he was also addressing himself to such academic subjects as the health of the arts, the origin of beauty, and the adequacy of various philosophical systems; despite the fact that he was filling his notebooks with lists of words whose precision, nuance, figuration, and musicality pleased his poetic sensibility; although he was jotting down minute descriptions of his observations of nature, and often when his eye was too full for words, he sketched this plenitude in a most stylized manner: his artistic personality was completely dominated by his concern for the condition and quality of his faith in God.

It is not surprising, then, that in his third year at Oxford, he experienced a religious crisis which caused him to appraise painfully his Anglican faith, only to discover that he could no longer hold it as truly Apostolic. Despite the pleas from his distinguished mentors, H. P. Liddon and E. B. Pusey, even with the disconcertment of his parents, which he termed, "terrible," he rushed to that English citadel of Rome, the Oratory of J. H. Newman.

There is much room for further biographical inquiry here. Something more surely can be said about the elements of his conversion. What prior influences did his friends have, such men as Dolben, Garrett, Macfarlane, and Addis? They were all religious enthusiasts of one sort or another. And what about two of his closest and dearest friends, Bridges and Baillie, who were skeptical of religion? And then there was the celebrated Regius Professor, W. Jowett, whose exhortations about the interpretation of biblical texts were about fifty years ahead of their time. Hopkins could have been inspired by this great scholar's turning his immense learning toward understanding the historical origins of Christianity through the same scholarly apparatus that he had employed in studying other Classical texts. Was Newman such an inspiration before Hopkins ever knew the man, that his own avidity for Classical scholarship had no bearing on his religious convictions? And the same might be said of Walter Pater who was then developing a rather intense and exciting humanistic philosophy. Hopkins shared a great many similar interests with both of these men, much of which he held on to even after his conversion and holy orders; yet they apparently never entered into those convincing arguments that made Newman chuckle during their first meeting.

Pondering Hopkins' later life, it is difficult not to think that they should have, for the scholar and the poet were later to weigh heavily on the priest as so many unfilled claims issuing from his nature and his education. The little consideration that these received before his conversion is a definite sign of the consuming singularity of his religious faith, a quality whose great asset was its genuineness, but whose great liability was its imprudence. A bit of a surprise can be detected in Hopkins' letter to Bridges[6] about his first visit to Newman. Newman was "unserious," and "genial"; he was solicitous for Hopkins' parents and thus urged him to delay being received--"...in no way did he urge me on, rather the other way." Hopkins was pleased and surprised at Newman's "interest and kindness" toward the Tractarians, his liberality toward the intellectual's difficulties with Catholicism. Newman's advice surely undercut the heroics of conversion: go back to school and get your degree and make a retreat to affirm your faith. Unfortunately, this calmness was short-lived.

The reactions at home threw him into a state of anxiety again. Apparently, he could not stand off for long the urgent appeals for him to desist for awhile.

His parents' reactions should not have been totally surprising. Hopkins remarked in a letter to Bridges, referred to above, that his parents might meet a mutual
acquaintance while abroad, an Edward W. Urquhart, who
was a private tutor for a time. "I hope they meet. My
mother, my brother says, has some prejudice about Urquhart, I conceive because he is looked upon as leading
me over to Rome." Hopkins' haste despite Newman's
counsels remains to be explained. We should like to
understand why his decision to act seemed so much more
firm than his convictions. Was it because he truly
feared the forces that might prevent him? Did he wish
to shut out any thought of familial betrayal? The possible implications here could bear heavily on the shape
of the rest of his life. Could it be that by this action he felt that he had to cut all those deeply shared
ties with his former life, ties allied with Anglican
Protestantism? He was now a missionary whose family,
friends, and acquaintances were the object of his mis-
sion.

It is not surprising that Hopkins immediately considered the religious life, if he felt that his conversion had cut him off from his normal relationships. After graduating in 1867 with a double first in Greats,
he accepted Newman's invitation to come to the Oratory
to teach in September. He found teaching wearisome and
was eager to get on with his religious vocation. In
January, he wrote to Bridges, who was then leaving on a
trip to Cairo, that he was on the brink of a major decision, that of taking religious orders. He was to ar-
rive at his final judgment "...by going into a retreat
at Easter at the latest...."[7] He left the Oratory in
April, 1868, on the twenty-seventh day of which he began his retreat at the Jesuit Novitiate. During this
time he decided to enter the Society of Jesus.

It will be hard for any biographer not to be puz-
zled by this choice unless he has been able to come up
with more evidence than is now available. At present
there is no evidence that Hopkins had had any contact
with the Jesuits. It is possible that he simply at-
tended a retreat at a time when he was on the brink of
this decision, and Father Henry Coleridge, S.J., who
gave the retreat, was so impressive that the Jesuits
somehow fulfilled Hopkins' buoyant missionary mood. To
a youth on fire with religious derring-do, the Jesuits
had the kind of lure that the French Foreign Legion has
for young military adventurers. This was especially
true in England where the Jesuits were either famous or

infamous from the days of Elizabeth I for their brilliance, dedication, and success. What outfit could be more appealing to a young, gifted, English rebel-convert?

Whatever the case, students of Hopkins are solely tempted to speculate on his suitability for the Jesuits. It is generally granted that he possessed the intellectual capacity and moral capacity, the dedication and the zeal. These he had in abundance. But what about his physical vigor and those necessary adaptive qualities required of a missioner (England was missionary territory)? And on what would that voracious artistic appetite feed among those plain and often bleak walls that house the order formed and fashioned by a soldier's sensibility? When Hopkins wrote to Newman of his acceptance by the Jesuits, he referred to the hard "Jesuit discipline." Newman replied with encouragement, and if he had any remorse for Hopkins' disinterest in the Oratorians, he did not show it. He closed by remarking, "The Benedictines would not have suited you."[8]

Any biographer will find it hard not to say something about this in the light of Hopkins' life in the Society. Besides a comparison of Benedictine monasticism and the Jesuit community, something undoubtedly will have to be said about the differences of spiritual discipline and cultural environment. Perhaps the Society's colder, driving intellectualism has something to do with Hopkins' turning to the warmer, affective theology of the Franciscan, John Duns Scotus, a theological system in which it might seem easier to be both a priest and a poet. Also, it is possible that the minimal communal life of the Society was behind Hopkins' undue reliance on guidance and permission from his Superiors. Maybe this is one reason why he felt such a failure in his vocation. He knew that he wanted more looking after than he should have. Moreover, he seems to have gotten more than his share anyway. It is strange to say this about such an innovating spirit as was Hopkins, for whom the free individuality allowed by the Society should have been entirely suitable, but enigmatically seemed not so. This is a major question for any Hopkins biographer. A case can be made that Newman was wrong about the Benedictines.

Of the number of questions still to be answered about the Jesuit years, none is more provocative than that of Hopkins giving up his writing. A biographer can hardly ignore a puzzle when his subject knowingly creates a serious problem for himself, wrestles with it

9

all his life, explains it to his friends, and dies, leaving it deliberately in a somewhat ambiguous state. Contrary to popular understanding, the writer's life was a problem before Hopkins ever had anything to do with the Jesuits. While at the Oratory, he wrote to his friend Baillie that at one time he wanted to be a painter, but "the higher and more attractive parts of the art put a strain upon the passions which I should think it unsafe to encounter."[9] Apparently, he felt that art was somehow incompatible with religion. It is possible, since he was here speaking of painting, that he was casting his Victorian eyes at contemporary French painting which seemed quite audacious to those times.

However, he did burn his poetry when he entered the Jesuit novitiate, an act that is more than full compliance with St. Ignatius' exhortation to enter "...with a large heart and with liberality towards his Creator and Lord, offering all his desires and liberty to Him, in order that His Divine Majesty may make use of his person."[10] Such a predisposition does not preclude literary talent as parts of the Bible make abundantly clear.

There is a pattern of thinking in Hopkins about religion and art which some modern readers find very attractive, which is that the true artist is by definition irreligious and/or antireligious. These weep over Hopkins as a martyr for poetry in the very citadel of the tyrant, the Society of Jesus. Eleanor Ruggles, who has written the latest biography of Hopkins (1944), seems to take this point of view: "For Hopkins knew that something of the artist's identity is consumed by his achievement. His passionate expression necessarily demands from him that self of self which God also demands and which, if it is to serve God unconditionally, must be directed toward Him alone."[11]

Now, if this messianic attitude were true, the biographer's problem would be largely to examine how religion got its destructive grasp on its artist-victim. However, the problem is infinitely more complex since religion is not intrinsically opposed to art as the history of world culture makes very clear, especially the Western tradition with its rich heritage of religious art. The only grounds for burning his poetry were his own special religious judgments. Catholicism and the Society of Jesus were simply the religious frame within which the judgment was made. It could have been any other sect of Christianity. Moreover, Hopkins could have carried on a literary career as a Jesuit religious, which could have been so managed that it could have strengthened his vocation where it needed it most: a sense of being professionally valuable to the Society. We can only speculate now, the originality of his art notwithstanding, as to what effect his poetic eloquence might have had on a suspicious England with its particular antipathies toward the Jesuits as well as the support panicky religious leaders would have received when his soaring affirmative, Christian testaments fell upon their Darwinized ears.

A well-known example today of what I am talking about would be Thomas Merton, who has joined a much stricter religious order than did Hopkins, and yet carries on a substantial literary career as a Trappist monk. History is replete with people who have been members of a religious order and at the same time been competent, even brilliant, successes in the major walks of life. Our expectations of true religion lead us to think of vocational enhancement rather than the inhibition of honorable human endeavors.

So the main sources of the priest-poet problem lay within Hopkins himself, and this is why it is a difficult, enigmatic, biographical issue. This is not to deny his Victorian mentality, nor to dismiss the fact that his perspectives were made more complex by his conversion and his religious vocation. These are important factors no doubt, but neither totally explains this central contrariety in his life.

Its centrality is indisputable. His letters and papers express over and over again that his deep desire to write was constantly before the tribunal of his conscience; that when he permitted himself greater freedom, he soon remorsefully rebuked himself; that he allayed his desires to some extent by engaging in a mostly literary correspondence with publicly recognized literary figures such as Bridges, Patmore, and Dixon, individuals who were actively engaged in letters and with whose interests he could vent his pent up creative surges. In each case, his manuscripts of poems, begrudgingly and spasmodically composed, were examined by each of these with considerable admiration. The inevitable question was posed: Why not publish them? In every instance, Hopkins, undoubtedly with the greatest self-control, replied that this could not be done for a number of reasons, the real one being this Gordian knot: I, a poet, became a priest, and thus should give up poetry. But you see, it is a very hard task.

The magnitude of this biographical question can be
appreciated if it is understood that this great issue
is the key to many other lesser problems during his
Jesuit years. While it is understandable, given his attitude, why he wrote so little poetry, and the kind he
did, his scrupulous attitudes must have been an influence on his shortcomings as a professional clergyman.
When one lists Hopkins' personal and professional qual-
ifications, it is evident from the record of his as-
signments that his superiors were hard put to make use
of his talents. I am astonished, personally, at the
tenderness with which he was treated--a quality normally
not associated with the Jesuit regimen.

Also, one cannot help but think that his preoccupation with this spiritual conflict must have influenced
his ability to write anything else. Although he had
envisioned at least five works, three in prose and two
in verse, these came to very little. And then there is
the question of his music. The new edition of Hopkins'
papers contains an essay on his compositions which consumed a good deal of his time and effort in his last
years. While it is true that his prosodic theories are
related to musical theory, and that mathematic progres-
sions of harmony were related to his philosophy of
beauty (he even expressed some of his sonnet forms in
fractions), one ponders whether what seemed a genuine
interest in music was not really a vicarious outlet for
the fierce frustration of the poet in him.

On considering the vast gamut of Hopkins' interests
at various periods of his life, ranging very nearly over
the whole area of the arts and sciences, dazzled by his
general intellectual brilliance in his correspondence
and his enormous fertility of mind in his notebooks, a
biographer is confronted by the mundane judgment that
this man frittered away his genius. So few men that
peopled Hopkins' time were his equal in mind, sensitivity, and creative talent, that it is accurate to say
that he brought into effective execution but a small
part of his personal power. Ungrateful though it
sounds, fourteen hundred lines of poetry, some of it
very exquisite poetry indeed, is a small voucher for the
creative force which signs indicate that this man had.

There is no reason to doubt that he was quite aware
of his powers. Time and again, when Bridges pronounced
a studied stricture about some poetic innovation, Hopkins explained in detail his artistic justification,
often in the most forthright language. He seldom
changed his mind. The tone of these passages, while

patient and indulgent for the most part, reveals a conscious superiority. However, these instances must be set against those in which Hopkins is slack and flat, wearied and distressed. These moments he was highly aware of also. Of course, this is more manifest in the Dublin years when he called this turn in his life "a lonely began," but he was summing up his life. And we must ponder his summation.

There are on hand a number of speculations about this central issue. And all of them can be fitted within the two basic orientations described at the beginning of this essay, the Religious and the New Critical. Those on the Religious side are nettled by any interpretation which places more emphasis on psychology than on Christian religion. They especially fear a Freudian point of view, which they see as implicit and unrestricted in the New Critical position, because such perspectives lead to unfounded judgments on Hopkins' psychic states without the informing context of his religion, and even worse, to egregious interpretations of his private spiritual notes, for example, the presence of a homosexual element, which cause unwarranted damage to Hopkins' reputation.

New Critics contend that textual evidence in much of Hopkins' poetry clearly shows that Hopkins became a psychoneurotic and that his case was increasingly worsened by some strange, inner drive to thrust his egomania into the suicide of a strongly abnegative religion. The result was the gradual annihilation of his personality, of which his poetry is an extraordinary verbal witness. They would counter the Religious position by noting that such an approach dismisses the findings of modern psychology, substituting for it a medieval explanation of the human personality, and worse, reads into the poetry this historical anachronism.

Despite the persistence that these two views are contradictory, I believe that both, with some modification, belong to Hopkins' story in a relation I have called tragicomic. While space forbids my taking every difference and demonstrating that separately each is part of a co-relative, perhaps one or two exhibitions will sketch what I mean.

One of the antagonisms is expressed as that of priest versus poet. Did the priest conflict with the poet? Dr. I. A. Richards believes so. Having concluded that the problem of poetic meaning is one in which psychology is "indispensable,"[12] the direction of his approach to this problem in Hopkins is clearly set by his conviction that religion and science must collide: "For it is no accident that Science and Religion conflict. They are different principles upon which impulses may be organized, and the more closely they are examined the more inevitable is the incompatibility seen to be."[13] Richards, whose article in *The Dial* (1926) was the first thorough analysis of some of Hopkins' poems from the New Critical point of view, and which later gave considerable impetus to "the problem of belief" in modern poetry, called the religious elements in Hopkins "bundles of invested emotional capital" making for his intellectual stiffness. He is then able to read the line from the sonnet, "The Windhover," "My heart in hiding Stirred for a bird,..." to mean that Hopkins was describing his *hiding* "from the life of the senses, from the life of the imagination and emotional risk, from speculation...hiding in the routine of meditation, in doctrine, etc...."[14] The poet is in frustrating collision with the priest.

Seven years later, Mr. Herbert Read[15] took the same view that poetic creativity in Hopkins was the result of a conflict between sensibility and belief. Thus he divided Hopkins' poetry into poems which express religious belief, those which have no relationship to belief at all, and those which express religious doubt. He saw in certain poems of the second category that "the poetic force comes from a vital awareness of the objective beauty of the world." He calls Hopkins' belated dedication, "To Christ our Lord" of "The Windhover" a sop to the poet's conscience. It is not surprising that he generally read Hopkins' poems as expressions of "faith tense but not firm," faith "held in opposition to his obstinate reasonings."

Hopkins' two biographers have taken the position that the priest converted the poet. His first biographer, G. F. Lahey, S.J., admits that during the last years in Dublin, Hopkins' physical frailness was at times inundated by his academic labors; further, he points to the sorrow Hopkins felt over the political atmosphere then in Dublin; however, he insists that a third sorrow which veined all of Hopkins' life, surfaced during his last years in Dublin, a suffering which "sprang from causes which have their origin in true mysticism. Hopkins, smiling and joyful with his friends, was at the same time on the bleak heights of

14

spiritual night with his God.... Hopkins was always remembered by all who met him as essentially a priest, a
deep and prayerful religious. With the fine uncompro-
mising courage of his initial conversion, he pursued his
never-ending quest after spiritual perfection. The celebrated 'terrible sonnets' are only terrible in the same
light that the beauty of Jesus Christ is terrible....
Read in this way his poems cease to be tragic."[16]

Some years later, his next biographer, Eleanor Ruggles, gave far more attention to Hopkins' personal problems. Despite her more comprehensive description of
his physical, psychological, and religious difficulties,
she still pictures him as an idealist who made an extra-
ordinarily valiant attempt to realize his high goals;
to her he was a missioner who unconditionally committed
himself to his faith with a Puritanically chaste dedication amidst many failures, fierce despairs, and para-
lyzing weaknesses. She comments that the measure of
his life rests on the Incarnation, as he himself in-
sisted. "This was always to be Hopkins' deepest realization and final comment."[17]

Now I submit that if the poet did not conflict with
the priest, Hopkins would not have become the kind of
priest he did--"a deep and prayerful religious." Yet,
if the priest had not converted the poet, the poet would
not have written the way he did--"...the desire to be an
artist and the desire to be a saint, was necessary to
his achievement as a poet."[18] Moreover, it is not necessary to do much guessing about the matter, for his
letters and papers ruminate over it. He could say to
E. H. Coleridge in 1866 while in the throes of his
conversion: "I think that the trivialness of life is,
and personally to each one, ought to be seen to be, done
away with by the Incarnation--or, I shd. say that difficulty wh. the trivialness of life presents ought to
be."[19] And he said to Canon Dixon in 1881, now having
tried assiduously to live according to this ideal:

When a man has given himself to
God's service, when he has denied himself
and followed Christ, he has fitted himself to receive and does receive from God
a special guidance, a more particular
providence. This guidance is conveyed
partly by the action of other men, as his
appointed superiors, and partly by direct
lights and inspirations. If I wait for such
guidance, through whatever channel conveyed,

about anything, about my poetry for instance, I do more wisely in every way than
if I try to serve my own seeming interests
in the matter. Now if you value what I
write, if I do myself, much more does
our Lord. And if he chooses to avail himself of what I leave at his disposal he
can do so with a felicity and with a success which I could never command.... This
is my principle and this in the main has
been my practice...but when one mixes with
the world...to live by faith is harder,
is very hard; nevertheless by God's help
I shall always do so.[20]

When a man is convinced that the Incarnation means
that the Infinite God became finite creature, that
Christ performed this "great sacrifice"[21] as a prototyp-
ical, perpetual act of divine love, then everything in
life takes on significance in terms of this ultimate
fact. Now if a mechanic or poet is so absolutely convinced, he might well deny all and give himself over to
God, but his vocational aptitude is still there and
yearns to be expressed. This is what Hopkins means when
he says that it is all "trivialness" from one point of
view--comedy, but "very hard" from another--tragedy.
Physical and psychological stress, of course, as well as
spiritual suffering are bound to occur. So are moments
of personal (poetic) equilibrium and religious joy.
These elements are alternately tragic and comic accord-
ingly whether you are taking the New Critical or Religious perspectives, and while each side talks as if the
other's alternative cannot be taken seriously, neither
side alone presents a case that assimilates all the
pertinent data. Nor can either, in my opinion, fully
read his poetry.

There is a passage in the private notes Hopkins
wrote while making a retreat at Beaumont during September, 1883, which underscores the paradox of the priest-
poet. While the priest had fervor, he could stand to
see the poet suffer and suffocate. But when he grew
tepid, as was to happen in Ireland, Hopkins seems to
have discovered a major spiritual resource in his writing. I think he dared hope for the first time in his
life that as a poet he could give himself to God. Maybe he did not have to burn his poetry, nor subdue his
inspiration; possibly he did not have to deny his personality to be a true religious. He wrote: "During this
retreat I have much and earnestly prayed that God will

16

lift me above myself to a higher state of grace, in
which I may have more union with him, be more zealous
to do his will, and freer from sin. Yesterday night it
was 15 years exactly since I came to the Society. In
this evening's meditation on the Temptation I was with
our Lord in the wilderness in spirit and again begged
this, acknowledging it was a great grace even to have
desire. For indeed it is a pure one and it is long
since I have had so strong and spiritual a one and so
persistent."[22]

Then what about his writing? That small, precious
collection he now saw as a gift to be given back to God,
from Whom, he now hopefully prayed, they ultimately
came. Those orphans, half-heartedly rejected by their
father and in the care of another man, are now reclaimed
and put in the care of the Lord. These are the tragicomic lines: "Also in some med. today I earnestly asked
our Lord to watch over my compositions, not to preserve
them from being lost or coming to nothing, for that I
am very willing they should be, but they might not do
me harm through the enmity or imprudence of any man or
my own; that he should have them as his own and employ
or not employ them as he should see fit. And this I
believe is heard."[23] The last line has taken on considerable significance since the day it was written.

However, there is that perennial tragic element
even in this religious franchise for his verse-writing,
which is, that his offering of the poetry he had already
written would have real spiritual merit if he now re-
nounced any future writing. But it was still hard for
him to eradicate a very natural bitterness. We can only
speculate how much this decision of the complete
sacrifice of his artistry had to do with that intense
depression he suffered during his last years in Ireland.
One is tempted to say that his poetic nature wreaked
its revenge. Whatever the source of his sorrows, this
disconsolate period is not without its comic aspects,
for it was during "that year of now done darkness" that
he resorted to his art with awful poetic results. While
he gave striking expression to the depths of his suffering, he likewise achieved poetic heights in uttering
that subtle, mysterious, onerous union between his will
and divine providence. In his last retreat notes just
before he died, and his letters as well, he makes frequent reference to "light" and "good spirits" though
his health grew worse. On his deathbed, he is reported
as having said, "I am so happy."

If, then, the priest-poet issue can be better understood from the broader vantage point of the tragicomic, it does so largely on biographical lines. But
does it make good sense of the historical milieu within
which Hopkins lived? Does it, for example, relate Hopkins' decidedly Victorian attributes with his Jesuit
way of life, or do we here find another conflict of the
priest-poet under a different guise?

Again the New Critical and the Religious positions
seem opposed. Mr. Arthur Mizener, for example, thinks
that Hopkins was "a Victorian with a special temperamen-
tal intensity of sensuous awareness and a special inclination toward that kind of asceticism which counter-
balances it."[24] He sees no real conflict between the
poet and the priest since Hopkins' basic sensibility was
Victorian, though "given a precision very nearly unique
for its time by a lifetime's habituation to scholastic
thought."[25] After reading the poems in the light of the
letters and papers, he comes to an inescapable conviction: "It is a conviction that Hopkins is Victorian, in
a good many respects obviously Victorian; and that it is
only the integrity and skill with which he fulfilled the
other impulses of his nature which tends to hinder our
recognition of the fact that even in these impulses he
represents his time."[26] The priest-poet conflict (or
conversion) dissolves under the heading "unique Victorian," but an immense amount of data withstands.

A contrary but related view with this New Critical
attitude is a theory suggested by Father Christopher
Devlin, S.J., editor of Hopkins' spiritual writings.
His speculation has to do with Hopkins and the Victorian
conscience. Taking his cue from the fact that Hopkins
preferred the theology of John Duns Scotus, a ninth-
century Franciscan, to that of Francisco Suarez, a sixteenth-century Jesuit, who was the currently accepted
theological guide of Hopkins' Jesuit superiors,[27] Father
Devlin speculates that one of the possible reasons for
this preference was that Hopkins' conscience was Victorian. More specifically, Hopkins may have placed a great
deal of reliance on Scotus' distinction between the
"elective will" and the "affective will," that is, the
affirmation of an inevitable opposition between choice
and desire. This emphasis seemed to give a theological
foundation to the standard predicament of the Victorian
conscience: duty is presumably contrary to wish in every
instance. It is this Victorian quality of Hopkins' conscience regarding his vocational duties which caused him
so much anguish over his desire to write. As a

consequence, "...Hopkins the Jesuit behaved to Hopkins
the poet as a Victorian husband might to a wife of whom
he had cause to be ashamed. His muse was a highborn
lady, a chaste matron, dedicate to God; but he treated
her in public as a slut, and her children as an unwanted
and vaguely sinful burden."[28] In this view, the major
bioqraphical problem is intricately tied up with Victorianism. It seems to leave out any Ignatian counterbalance, however.

On the Religious side, we have posed against the
Victorian mind that of the Ignatian tradition of spirituality. The point of view is stated clearly by the
distinguished Hopkins scholar, W. H. Gardner: "Whoever
would understand Hopkins must go not to Freudian psychology but rather to the 'Spiritual Exercises' of St.
Ignatius Loyola, the founder of the Society of Jesus.
Loyola was a great psychologist, and the religious
values for which he and his disciple Hopkins stood have
never been confuted, though they have often been rejected or ignored."[29]

Specifically, it is argued that it was Ignatian
spirituality by means of which Hopkins was able to fuse
the priesthood with his poetic genius, the result of
which is the finest religious verse since the Meta-
physicals. This main argument was first made by Dr.
John Pick who stressed the centrality of the Spiritual
Exercises: "For twenty-one years Hopkins dedicated himself to the Society of Jesus; for twenty-one years he
studied, meditated, and practiced the Spiritual Exercises. They became part of his life and attitude. They
gave direction to all he experienced, thought, and
wrote.... Without knowing something of them we can
hardly know the priest-poet."[30]

Again, I submit that a tragicomic approach would
meaningfully fuse all of these perspectives. In a study
of the Ignatian influence on Hopkins,[31] I have suggested
that Hopkins' Victorian mind and conscience, his preference for Scotus, and the Ignatian discipline all meet
in Hopkins' own experience with the tradition of Christian asceticism. Hopkins' life-long melancholia and
his precocious, ascetic predispositions were fed by
those aspects of Christian mortification that especially
typify the first thousand years of Christianity, beginning with St. Paul and extending through the Patrisitc
tradition up to and until Anselm. Ignatius came into
contact with this tradition through Kempis' *Imitation of
Christ*, much of the spirit of which he put into his

Exercises. However, I propose that Ignatius considerably modified the assumption in Kempis that Christian perfection demands total rejection of this life. Rather, Ignatius stipulated, Christian perfection demands proper use of creatures in its attainment (a principle which has a great deal to do with the success of the Society of Jesus, in my opinion). Consequently, spiritual consolation is the normal and desired state, and disconsolation a state considered abnormal and undesirable unless of mystical origin. This is quite clear in the Exercises.

Hopkins, of course, came to the earlier ascetical tradition largely through the Exercises, but for some set of tragicomic circumstances involving all the possibilities aforementioned, he was unable, during most of his life, to follow his spiritual guide in the matter of his artistic desires and his spiritual welfare. He seems somewhat pre-Ignatian on this count, as if Loyola had not modified Kempis at all. In this attitude is present also that intransigent, categorical morality of Calvinism which, as we noted earlier, fretted Victorian Protestantism, one of the qualities that made English converts to Catholicism suspicious to the Continentals. Even Newman experienced this as is apparent in his relations with the Vatican.[32]

So Hopkins' Victorian temperament, partially affirmed in early Christian asceticism, sharpened by his interest in Scholastic thought, but counterbalanced by his attempt to relate Scotistic theology to the Ignatian discipline, led him along a winding and thorny path of self-rejection and religious crises, which, with his irrepressible creativity, resulted in some of the rarest poetic art in English letters. The comic climax to his tragedy of frustration and sacrifice is his grand personal reconciliation begun during his retreat at Beaumont (1883), though the beautiful record of it all was not to be made public for over a third of a century and in another century.

Modern biography must be multidimensional not only because we have developed so many anatomies, but also because man is bigger than them all. Hopkins is a case in point, but this is not the only reason that warrants the scope of tragicomedy. The latent shape of his life is in his poetry: the "sheer plod makes plough down sillion/Shine...." It is the paradox of the "plod" of tragedy and the "Shine" of comedy that makes Hopkins' life so memorable and his poetic art so vital to us.

No sensitive reader can but feel his pluck at the deeper
strings of things--the blunt, painful imponderables of
existence and the sudden, mysterious sense of the
rightness of life.

However, we need to complete the historical frame
which maps all valuable human utterance. Biography is
a necessary adjunct to historical criticism just as the
latter is a requisite to understand an act of language.
A sampling of recent essays on Hopkins makes it very
clear that textual analysis is badly in need of a definitive biographical guide. Scholarship on Victorian Hopkins is somewhat in the same state as much of that on
Joyce before Ellman's biography: brilliant suggestions
and ingenious possibilities. The lasting word awaits
the fullness of historicity.

II

Such was the status of Hopkins' biography over
twenty years ago, and astonishingly it still is the
case today. A little updating makes my essay as current as it was in 1961.

Amid many essays offering biographical perspectives, there has been only one serious effort at a complete biography, that written by Bernard Bergonzi,[33]
and a longer but foreshortened effort by Paddy Kitchen.[34] Neither book breaks any new ground either with
fresh information or original insight into Hopkins'
life. Kitchen calls her book a "personal" life and Bergonzi tells us at the outset that there is nothing new
about Hopkins in his effort. Until a more "definitive"
biography is written, we must wait for a deeper understanding of Hopkins' family heritage, finer presenta-
tions of Kate and Manley Hopkins, a solid awareness of
Hopkins' childhood, and much needed clarifications to
background the family response to Gerard's conversion
and having a Jesuit in the family.

The dearth of complete biographies does not mean
that biographical interest in Hopkins has been lacking
the past twenty years. In fact quite the contrary is
true. Several facets of Hopkins' life have received a
good deal of attention.

The most notable, and to my mind, important biographical contribution is Alfred Thomas' treatment of
Hopkins' years in training as a Jesuit.[35] Fr. Thomas
actually performed a double service to Hopkins

scholarship. First he provides in his book a picture of life in the Society of Jesus in such great and accurate detail that anyone interested in the kind of training and activities, or the quality of life which Hopkins lived after entering the Society, cannot help but obtain a fresh understanding of what it meant to live a Jesuit life in Victorian England. Second, the book provides so many explicit particulars about Hopkins' life as a novice through his years as a tertian (final vows) that the reader vicariously lives the daily regimen of the Jesuit along with Hopkins. How amazingly simple and ordinary it all was on the outside in contrast to the "war within." A future writer of a complete biography will have to insert much of Thomas' book because Hopkins' Jesuit years have been so completely accounted for.

Alison Sulloway has given us some valuable insights to Hopkins' Oxford years. By recalling the character of an Oxford education in the 1860s, she provides interesting and useful awarenesses of the temper of life into which Hopkins was immersed, some insight into the pattern of Hopkins' response to Oxford life, backgrounding his conversion. Her book is specially useful in understanding the shaping of Hopkins' esthetic ideals and values from his admiration and acceptance of the artistic attitudes of John Ruskin. Hopkins' complete biographer will be aided by Sulloway's examination of Hopkins' Victorian temper. Fr. Michael Allsopp has added two informative examinations of what Hopkins experienced in his formal studies at Highgate and Oxford,[37] while Francis Keegan has supplied a detailed picture of Mt. St. Mary's in Hopkins' time. Gerald Roberts has provided a similar effort on Stonyhurst.[38] Thus period studies (plus pictorial portraits)[39] have emerged to sharpen our biographical knowledge of Hopkins' life.

People in Hopkins' life have received attention in the scholarship of the last two decades. Jean-George Ritz examined Robert Bridges and his friendship with Hopkins.[40] This relationship, of course, is a major question in Hopkins' scholarship and surely must receive extensive treatment in any complete biography. Ritz' portrayal of the association is informative, his reflection of the two personalities detailed, but he never arrives at an adequate assessment of the friendship so that the major questions on the minds of Hopkins' students get answered. These questions, answered one way, amount to a conspiracy theory in which Bridges, a

22

second-rater compared to Hopkins, blustered and blundered in trying to cope with the spiritual purity and poetic genius of his friend Hopkins, misunderstood his poetic genius and was baffled by his poetry; he found his own intellectual and cultural narrowness challenged, knew his own poetry inferior and his own critical accumen overmatched. In such circumstances of apparent superiority, but real inferiority, Bridges bluffed it out, cribbed ineffectually for his own poetic reputation, and was left with an overwhelming question: Should he keep from the world the art of a poetic genius? After cutting all his possible losses (collecting all his letters so far as possible and destroying them as well as insisting that no biography be written of himself), Bridges, to his credit, at long last, gave Hopkins to the world. This view, shocking to many, is seriously held by informed Hopkins scholars of my acquaintance. Unfortunately, Mr. Ritz does not counter or affirm these serious allegations. In my reading, Ritz' study intensifies these burning questions. Neither of the recent biographies on Hopkins grapples with this important question. The safe response is gratitude that Bridges saw to it that Hopkins was published at all. To have done otherwise, however, would have been monstrous and no one, not even the most anti-Bridges Hopkins student, casts Bridges in this light. In fact, if the above allegations contain some truth, some sympathy is called for. How difficult it must have been for an arrogant, frequently imperious, often rude person (as pictured by Ritz) to have to confront the intensity of spirit, mind, goodness, and talent of a Gerard Hopkins. You need not have been a "run of the mill poet," which Bridges was not, to have found trouble in such a friendship.[41] Donald E. Stanford's book on Bridges' poetry stresses the classical mode of Bridges' literary art.[42] Hopkins saw this as the chief characteristic of Bridges' work and told him so in 1880. The wonder is whether he would have the same enthusiasm for Bridges' style had he lived long enough to read Bridges' later poetic efforts in a more colloquial poetic mode. My guess is that Hopkins honestly admired Bridges' traditional manner but knew in his poetic heart that his "classic" style was dead; so did Bridges later as he ruminated over the precious scrapbook of poems of his dead Jesuit friend. How difficult it must have been for him to watch his own poetry become passé and Hopkins' increasingly current!

Another important and interesting figure in Hopkins' life was Walter Pater. There has been no full-scale treatment of Hopkins' association with Pater since my own study in 1965.[43] Of course, since this time, Hopkins has figured in general treatments of Pater. In critical studies of Hopkins, the possible influence of Pater upon Hopkins' theory of artistic form has received mixed attention. John Robinson[44] makes this topic a major concern, but Elizabeth Schneider mentions Pater once, for example. In his biography, Bergonzi brings up Pater in a routine biographical presentation and goes no further than standard speculations about the relationship. The last word has probably not been said about this unusual esthetic and religious kinship.

Among Hopkins' Oxford friends, only Digby M. Dolben has received any detailed attention. In fact Dolben has become what one might term a "hot" discussion in Hopkins scholarship mainly because of the readiness these days to be open about homosexuality and the supposed boldness attained by suggesting that the brilliant, Victorian, Jesuit poet might have been an homosexual.[45] Bergonzi gives more attention to Dolben than any of Hopkins' friends and Paddy Kitchen has virtually written her whole biography around her interest in homoeroticism in Hopkins' life and work. Gay readers of Hopkins purport to find their own erotic leanings in his poems.

First of all, there is no hard evidence to date that D. M. Dolben had anything but a brief association with Hopkins. Apparently Dolben was a talented but very strange young man whose untimely accidental death leaves very little to be said about him or any relationships he might have had. Therefore any discussion of a possible homosexual relationship between Dolben and Hopkins must rest upon wholesale fabrication.

Second, no special tendencies are particularly traceable to Hopkins' private confession notes just because they reflect that he was struggling for moral control over his own sexual feelings, or that he associated his enormous attraction to beauty with possible sexual lures. After all, what was to be expected of him going through puberty? What is important in these notes is not that he experienced nocturnal emissions, felt the growing powers of his sexual energies, even perhaps masturbated at times; what is important are his efforts to achieve and maintain a purity of mind and body commensurate with his own piety and moral idealism. This is to say nothing more than that the confession notes he kept were meant to be aids to his reclaiming and

maintaining sexual purity in his life. To scan them
for other reasons is to make worse the modern penchant
for the violation of personal privacy.

However the topic of homosexuality and Hopkins
still persists. John Robinson sees in Hopkins' frequent depiction of boys and men as beautiful a betrayal
of homosexual feelings in him "whose presence is, in
my view, conclusively established by his unpublished
confession-notes."[46] In his reference, Robinson states
that he sees homosexual feeling in them despite the
fact they are confession notes. He goes on to dwell
on passages in Hopkins' poems wherein he depicts male
beauty, the spiritual and incarnational implications
in the texts notwithstanding.

Twenty-six years ago, when I was writing my dis-
sertation on Hopkins for the late American poet, Theodore Roethke, I had a two-hour discussion with him about
Hopkins in general and his writing in particular. The
topic of homoerotic images came up to which Roethke
made a very considerable response. He noted that there
is such a very strong emphasis in Hopkins' poetry and
wondered why. In those days homosexuality in Hopkins
was barely mentionable, but I brought up the possibility. Roethke said there was nothing in Hopkins' life
to admit of such an inclination. I mentioned his association with Pater, his meeting with Simeon Soloman
("Who the hell was he?" Roethke growled softly), and
the homoerotic tendencies in British schools. He dis-
missed such speculative meandering out of hand and remarked that what is important is what is in the poetry
and what is there is a strong feeling for manliness,
an astonishingly accurate eye for the human anatomy,
and a wondrous feel for maleness. Was this not homosexual feeling? No, he replied; it was damn cunning of
Hopkins to spot in Romantic poetry its feminine character, that is, its tendency towards the delicate image
and/or the engagement with the softer side of human
emotion, and see the need to rebalance the imagination
on the masculine side.

These remarks have lain hidden in my recollections
of my association with Roethke until I began to address
the current attitudes about homoeroticism in Hopkins'
poetry--the only place where the topic is even discuss-
ible. What are the implications of manliness and Romanticism? As a Romantic, Hopkins felt the pull of the
feminine sensibility in his "inscaping" of experience.
This feminization of awareness, F. X. Shea has pointed
out, is consistent with the emphasis in Romanticism on

experience which in its religious phase means a concentration on rite, sacrament, and spiritual transport.[47]
Hopkins saw, in seeking a new expression of religious experience, that just as the old tradition of faith (Rationalism) unbalanced the religious consciousness in favor of conceptualization, logical analysis, and doctrine, the masculine ideal, so Romanticism caused unbalance in the other way of felt experience without rational centers. The true character of higher Romanticism, Hopkins understood, is epicene. Thus, in his own restructuring of what he called a "new Realism" both the Rationalist and the Romantic factors have to be wedded in a new identity. In fact in his century the Romantic, human model had been given an overly feminine quality in fierce opposition to the forces of scientific and technological Rationalism raging throughout Western culture. This rebalancing effort meant reclaiming some of the masculine tone and value of traditional Rationalism, for example, its intellectual toughness and its conceptual grasp, without giving up the Romantic, feminine quality of openness to experience, emotional depths, and intuitive visions. In effect Hopkins judged the separation of the two cultural ideals as signs of a cultural fracture in the minds and hearts of Western humanity. The two sexual cultures, his position stresses, need to be unified. The touchstone of such a unified consciousness was what he called "manly tenderness," a quality he thought necessary to all truly balanced life and art.

Now without denying that Hopkins stresses male beauty in his poetry (a quality I might add, surely influenced by his chosen state in life, specially his religious ideal, Christ, whom all his spiritual mentors exhorted him to imitate down to the most specific of details), I suggest that what in some modern readers' experience seems "homosexual feeling" is a mistaking of the significance of "manly tenderness." As a Romantic, Hopkins did not want his art to have the conventional weaknesses of much of the poetry of his Romantic contemporaries, subjective feminine softness without the tensile strength of objective concepts. He sought in his poetic characterizations of people this epicene quality as he attempted to give everything he wrote tough-mindedness and fine feeling. This artistic ideal is apparent in his work almost from the beginning. Take "the tall nun" in *The Wreck*, for instance. As a woman she is open to the dread and horror of the tragedy she is experiencing; moreover, she is, at another level, totally docile to the religious character of her

26

experience of the shipwreck. Hopkins made of her his
kind of Romantic heroine; open to all that tragic human
suffering, still she had that sense of rational command
to see that in the very torrent and toils of her predicament her whole life's vocation was being brought to
judgmental significance. In her trials, he had to find
that enabling grace to render this event "rational" at
a very high level of spiritual meaning and find the
courage to correspond. I think Hopkins was trying to
express "manly tenderness" in the actions and awarenesses of the "tall nun": "Well, there was a heart
right!/ There was a single eye!/ Read the unshapeable
shock night/ And knew the who and the why." In Hopkins'
Romantic conception of her, she is fully open to the
total experience of her human fate yet she is able to
drive through the storm toward some transcendent consciousness. Her calling out for an ultimate reprieve
in the press of her dire predicament represents an enormous courage to transport herself to the highest levels
of consciousness her religious experience will take
her. Her being thronged with a thousand feelings, she
was able to penetrate her experience in the night roar:
"a lioness arose"; "...she rears herself to divine/Ears,
and the call of the tall nun/ To the men in the tops and
tackle rode over the storm's brawling." I think this
heroic figure is truly expressive of Hopkins' artistic
ideal of "manly tenderness" and symbolic of his own
personal, religious idealism. Also we must not forget
how deeply Hopkins felt and shared the religious experience and faith-mindedness of women--Jesus' mother,
Marie Lataste, St. Winefred, Margaret Cliteroe, St.
Dorothea. Women were very strong attractions to Hopkins' religious and poetic personality.

"Manly tenderness" then is sensitivity to and
awareness of the affective element in human experience
as well as openness to be transported to higher levels
of consciousness, mental and moral, to love and be loved
feelingly and knowingly at some very sublime level beyond ground level experience, "Yonder." Hopkins beautifully captures these qualities of his Romantic "manly
tenderness" in language which conveys the feminine passion of lover and mother side by side with the more
sinewy language of masculine courage and fealty in
facing death. The key to "manly tenderness" is language, the creative ability to "heighten" words in different gender directions at the same time maintaining
the immediacy of an unique individual voice, a highly
individualized speech.

"Manly tenderness" describes Felix Randal, Harry Ploughman, Tom and Dick in "Tom's Garland," and the soldier in the poem of the same name.[48] Felix, "big-boned and hardy-handsome," weeps over his illness like a sick child, and while the poet remembers him as the epitome of the manly, "powerful amidst peers," he is described as a maker of sandals evoking delicacy, sensitivity, and feeling. The code of the soldier is a manly idealism: "Here it is: the heart,/ Since, proud, it calls the calling manly, gives a guess/ That, hopes that, makesbelieve, the men must be no less...." But the poet notes just as he is the model in all things, Christ is the model for the soldier. In Him is the scarlet spirit of war as well. But also in the Christ-model is loving tenderness, "For love he leans forth ...." So manly tenderness is the true "inscape" of the soldier.

The same combination of masculine toughness softened by a tender spirit is apparent in "Harry Ploughman." Manliness in this poem is depicted in a vivid word picture of a classic physique hewn of the earth's environment. The poem virtually sculpts out in the vein of the monumentality of Michelangelo Harry's extraordinary bodily attributes--arms, chest, and legs. Then the picture of him is animated carrying on his characteristic task, ploughing, as if his actions and motions were a dance of work. The marvelous harmony and rhythm which this beautiful body possesses are expressed by the poet in the play of the head, the color changes in the face, and the sway of the hair. Through the heightened language the gender direction chan es from manly size and hardness to tender lightness and delicateness--"Hard as hurdle arms" to "wind-lilylocks-laced." The last lines rest this poetic sculpture on the Ploughman's booted feet dancing in all this "Churlsgrace" of "manly tenderness," a word picture of power and delicacy. I suggest there is an epicene character in Harry, a depiction that attempts to realize both the male and female qualities actually in human nature, selved uniquely in this man and "inscaped" by the poet. Those readers who claim to detect homosexual feelings in such descriptions in Hopkins are mistaking male sexuality for unisexuality. At their best and most balanced, poems like these in Hopkins' canon are an epithalamion celebrating the marriage of masculine and feminine elements in the human consciousness.

The Romantic ideal of "manly tenderness," which I see as an important element in Hopkins' "new Realism,"

is not always nor easily balanced with actual experience. There are moments of unbalance in Hopkins' poetry in which manliness dominates in the form of cold, heartless reason abstracting the human predicament into categories of good or bad, right or wrong, beautiful or ugly, saved or damned. Christianity can be reduced to a debit-credit system of accounting conduct in terms of moral arrears and sinful bankruptcy. From the beginning, there was the tendency in Hopkins to be audit-minded about moral life, a religious quality encouraged by his Protestant, religious mentors and never radically altered by his Catholic directors. In his letters and notebooks as well as in his poems, Hopkins at times is prone to make somewhat righteous, doomsday judgments of the natural and the human worlds. In saying this we must keep in mind the difficult paradox the ardent Christian tries to live and practice, namely, that one must hate sinfulness yet forgive the sinner, a psychomoral juxtaposition requiring the greatest mental-moral agility within the personality. There is the strongest inclination for those with the highest personal, moral ideals to resolve the ambiguity of sin in simplistic, elective solutions.

Anyone who knows Hopkins' life and work cannot help but be aware of the great idealism of morality and holiness which permeated his life. His extraordinary moral and religious expectations of himself made him all the more susceptible to stereotypical lapses of judgment about the sinful ways of the world. However, for a Christian, Romantic writer with such strong ethical tilts, Hopkins' writing is in the main remarkably morally poised and balanced in its ethical perspective. Seldom does his rich religious sensibility succumb to an easy judgment of the moral dilemma of evil. For the most part, Hopkins remains true to the basic Christian attitude that Divinity is locatable in Nature and human nature, that living the Christian life means trying to see Christ in the sinner, failing to do so and having to start over, relying on, asking for, and cooperating with whatever aid (grace) that comes from the outside. This is the daily bread of Christian living.

As a priest, Hopkins discovered to his sorrow, irritation, even anger, that far too many human beings, even Christians, remain obtuse to any vital, religious dimension in human experience and hence are mostly indifferent to the kinds of life choices devout Christians should make. Thus the prime challenge to Christian witnesses such as priests, whose vocation is to bring about

religious awareness in the daily life experiences of
people, is to awaken the spiritual mind. In his work
as a priest, Hopkins, of course, took up this task with
great earnestness. He soon found how heavy a burden
this priestly duty is, how frustrating and how debili-
tating. When coupled with his own personal, religious
failures, unsurprisingly, at times, his normally balanced view of the moral and religious lives of people
could become judgmental rather than loving, categoriz-
ing rather than forgiving. At such moments Christian
love diminishes, and if you are a Christian religious
poet, such lapses may be "inscaped."

Hopkins' poem "Tom's Garland" is one of these unbalanced moments in his religious sensibility. The
poem as I read it, depicts the common laborer as a very
low level of human life, little more than an animal,
with a human personality diminished to the lowest common denominator. To be sure, Tom's human state is much
involved in the conditions of social injustice, but his
limitations—denseness, ignorance, and insensitivity—
are partial personal qualifiers for his underclass status. His needs are basic, to be sure generally human;
nevertheless bed, bread and his work comprise an existence at the biological level. Tom feels no kinship to
any more humanizing class; a laborer, he does the
world's brute work. Take this away and he is destroyed.
He cannot move into another world. Dumb, unsustained,
reduced to the basic biological instincts for life,
Tom and his brethren can become like packs of ravenous
dogs or wolves scavenging the streets and alleys of the
world in search of their elemental securities. Gar-
landed only with care, despair, dullness, and rage, Tom
and his like trample the world in their steel-treaded
boots ransacking wherever they go—manwolves. Tom, the
navvy, becomes Tom, the Manwolf. The poem is full of
warning, dread and fear over human nature turned bes-
tial. Nor is there a shred of "manly tenderness" in
Tom or his "inscaper." The poem is brutally objective,
frank, and factual. No transcendental perspectives,
Christian or otherwise, are offered in the poem. The
poetic eye is pitiless and the poetic heart unfeeling
except perhaps for fear.

"The shepherd's brow"[49] is another poem lacking
the balance of Christian "manly tenderness." Written
in those years of his life when his Christian, priestly-
poetic balance was in its greatest peril, Hopkins expressed his bitterest estimate of humanity. In the
first part of the poem, he notes, to the disparagement
of puny, rebellious mankind, what real rebellion is—the

angels' disobedient battle with God. Then he turns to
the weakling condition of man's disobedience. From a
kind of Miltonic height, Hopkins peers upon the fragility, helplessness, and animality of the human condition
to pronounce it pitiful, trivial, and sordid. Human
self-pride is scorned, and human love is put down as a
form of impurity. The "inscaping" is one of harsh judgment, full of belittling and discounting feelings. The
picture of the human race is a sour one without any trace
of Christian sympathy or forgiveness. Human beings are
touched with no manly handling or feminine tenderness.
The poet seems to realize his unbalance, for in the last
lines he acknowledges his black mood, his mordant feelings, his disordered sensibility, which have so unhinged
his view of things. Still the reader feels that the
poet has been more than "fussy" in his depiction, a word
that seems too weak to carry the heavy judgments laid
upon us all. The poem's powerful contrasting of the
giant angels with dwarfed human nature, the attack upon
the human personality, and the accusation of "dirtiness"
in human love--these diminishments do powerfully rack
the reader so that the poet's explanation at the end of
the poem, at the most, only partially soothes us, only
begins to rebalance perspective, and does not wash away
our felt bitterness and disgust. The Olympian view, as
always, suffers and succumbs to the great risk of final
alienation.

   I accept the fact that when a genuine and powerful
Romantic, Christian sensibility feels thwarted, it can
become especially aggravated when confronting the in-
veterateness of human weakness, or when human nature
seems unable to penetrate beyond its own natural pro-
clivities. In these instances the negative field of
forces felt often cannot be overcome; the aspiring,
spiritualizing consciousness seems unable to rise above
the disintegrative powers in things and people. Inevi-
tably, if one is moved to expression, statements result
which are a falling back into a dejected and jaded state
rationalized by casting pejorative judgments upon nature's naturalness and human nature's moral intransi-
gence. Life is made up of these zigzags in consciousness; it is the desire of Christians to handle them with
Christian understanding. Often, however, a balanced and
forgiving perspective about life and people is very difficult to maintain specially when one's motivation is
encumbered by one's own, felt failures, the pervasive-
ness of personal sin and the wavering of personal will.
Such trials are the hair shirt of any Christian
disposition.

31

In Hopkins' case, the question is whether in these "contending" poems, the poet is really rebelling or mainly "inscaping" the human experience of spiritual discontent. Many readers of "Thou are indeed just," "The shepherd's brow," and "The fine delight" take them as unqualified poetic statements of Hopkins' vocational unhappiness and spiritual frustration. Read as single-minded complaints, these poems take on the air of a contentious "falling out" with God. But in the final critical analysis this is a silly critical response, first, because to someone who truly recognizes and accepts the Deity as the "lord of life," the apparent maladjustment of justice on the human scale is of little consequence, and second, in each of these poems the dominating element in the "inscaping" is not spiritual contentiousness, which is surely there, but rather the deep sense of God's awful power and the mystery of its purpose before which it is vain and presumptuous to complain. While it is proper, just, and right to plead before the God "that hews mountain and continent,/Earth, all, out..." for a change in spiritual climate, it is not proper to play angry God outraging oneself, disremembering that life after all is, by definition, a poor reflection of the Divine image, as the poet himself notes in his spoons image. Finally, "The fine delight" and the "Sweet fire," Hopkins explains to Bridges, has its seasons, and though the "winter world...scarcely breathes that bliss," still they inspire enough to create this beautiful explanation. Careful reading of these "contentious" poems, then, reveals the very human side of the poet as the "just man justices;/Keeps grace: that keeps all his goings graces...."[50]

However it is fair to read these poems as expressions of a very different spirituality than Hopkins had ever expressed before. There are evidences in the poems, which biography soundly supports, that indicate the severe spiritual trials which Hopkins' religious consciousness underwent. The religious states depicted in these poems, however, are part of the continuing development of Christian mindedness and spirituality; they are not spiritual breakdowns, but breakthroughs to greater and richer religious consciousness. This point is especially underscored by the fact that Hopkins' creative, Romantic imagination found it possible to "inscape" these religious states of consciousness, these experiences of "dark" graces, with as much power and perfection as he was able earlier to produce poems expressing the luminescenses of "light" graces.

John Robinson sees such religious experience in Hopkins not as a stage of development, but as an "oscillation" indicating Hopkins' failure to "interiorize" his Catholic Christian faith.[51] The reason he offers for these swings is that Hopkins was able to love the human person only in "primal innocence."[52] There is no doubt that Hopkins had to struggle to achieve a maturely Christian estimate of the human condition, moral and otherwise; additionally he had to fight to maintain that Christian spiritual and moral equilibrium in which one hates sin but loves the sinner. "Manly tenderness" as an esthetic equivalent is even harder to balance, specially when the inspiration for it gets jumbled. No one can perpetually maintain absolute spiritual equilibrium in one's religious consciousness, such is human frailty. Robinson is right about stressing such failures as unChristian. He is wrong, however, about the implications of such a religious mentality. To an aspiring Christian consciousness such as Hopkins possessed, the difference between the promises of Christ and secularism is literally the difference between doom and glory, as Hopkins uncompromisingly stated it time and again, specially if you have and hold the kind of Christian assent which Hopkins possessed. Thus Hopkins was pledged by mind, imagination, vocation, life itself, to sound the huge difference between "for" Christ or "against" Christ. Surely it is understandable that such a deeply devout, religious personality would constantly place the highest regard on the "next world," would be always aware of "the fragility and vacuity" of the human community, would be painfully in touch with the bottomless pit of human selfishness, "man so intent on himself." Mired and moiled in the calamity of human history, each human being needs to hear the good news of Christian destiny which as a Christian priest Hopkins was bound to preach. As a poet whose imagination was primarily shaped by his Christian consciousness and experience, of course, he would seek to express the transporting vision of Divinity in real experience. For these Christian mentalities, perspectives, actions, expressions, Robinson castigates Hopkins. The poems of religious transport Robinson reads as the expressions of a "wistful" solitary; "God's Grandeur," for example, he reads as "whimsicality...jerked into a token service of his faith." Such expressions, he argues, are religious "fancifulness" and naiveté," "religion in magical terms." This is secular criticism failing to come to grips with genuine religious poetry of a very high order.[53] Clearly this reader has little sympathy for poetry of religious transport, apparently no

motivation to suspend his disbelief to try to reach the
level of religious imagination expressed in the poetry,
no personal ability to take in, even in the esthetic
mode, intimations of a very transcendent, spiritual significance. To such readers, Christian Romanticism is
bogus because it pretends, or worse, "believes" in the
authentication of Christ in real experience. To the
secularist imagination, in those moments when the poet
finally moves out of his "wistfulness" and sees the
world for what it is, he becomes "rational" and "realis-
tic," is able to express the authentically real human
condition--"womb-to-tomb." Readers of Hopkins like
Robinson interpret his last poems as poems of awakening
in which the poet had to grow up by dying to the death
of his hopeless, spiritual idealism. Unlike the earlier
poems of imaginative fakery, illusioned by sentimental-
ity and confessional rant, the later poems are hard,
tough, true and hence more convincing. These are the
only poems in Hopkins' canon which secular-minded
readers like Robinson can truly relate to because they
are the only poems which Hopkins wrote which are susceptible to secularist mentalities. The earlier poems
face the reader with unabashed celebrations of "Christ-
scapes" in the real world; take it or leave it, that's
what they talk about. The secular imagination must
suspend real engagement with these poems and talk about
other things like elision or linguistic extravagance in
Hopkins. However the poems of negative religious experience can be psychologized into modern secular terms
and attitudes, reduced to the couch, so to speak, and
because of this translation, they become accessible to
secularist meanings and responses. I do not condemn
readers like Robinson because of their un-Christian consciousness, for their inability to have esthetic intimation of the deific experience, the "beyond," the transfigured. I realize that religious consciousness is a
condition of faith inwardly sorting experience for instances of Divinity, a spiritual state not in the possession of every human being. I also realize that not
all Christians truly have such faith nor do all believers of any faith. However, I do think it necessary
that such readers face up to the authors they read. In
Hopkins' case, this means trying to see objectively the
phenomenology of his religious experience in his poetry,
acknowledging its authenticity however beyond the ken of
one's own experience it is, and in transposing the poetry into alien mentalities of acceptable personal
readership, to admit the "misreading" taking place, misreading which may have some justification from a certain
critical point of view but misreading nevertheless. Unfortunately these clarifying, critical honesties have

not been adequately stated in Robinson's treatment of
Hopkins leaving the unaware reader with the impression
that there are not fundamental collisions of values and
attitudes between his secular, materialist critiques and
those of Romantic Christians. Robinson's chapter titled, "Eternal May-time" is a brilliant example of this
critical confusion.[54]

Moreover in this chapter there is a more serious
issue raised, that of the integrity of Hopkins' spirituality, a topic surely to be a major subject in any
"definitive" biography. Robinson argues very strongly
in his chapter that Hopkins' Christian Catholicism was
largely exterior, that Hopkins failed to interiorize the
doctrines of his belief, "and this seems to me his
severest limitation as a poet." Robinson contends that
Hopkins couldn't bear to see ugliness, moral or esthetic, in the beauties of this world and so was tossed
about between his emotional commitment to beauty and
innocence and ugliness (natural evil) and sin. Hopkins'
spiritual ambivalence constantly wrenched his poetry into poetic contortions which reveal his airy, dreamy,
Romantic Christianity on the one hand and his moral
cynicism on the other. Robinson comments: "Between the
romanticism of holding the one and the cynicism of
holding the other as the sole and all-inclusive truth
lies the wisdom." Clearly such a critical attitude has
enormous implications for any biographer of Hopkins and
major consequences for any critic of his poetry.

My own response to Robinson's view (and he should
be credited for openly and forthrightly stating his
reservations about Hopkins' spirituality) is that he has
not grasped how deeply Christian is the religious experience expressed in Hopkins' poetry. Moreover he has
not seen that Hopkins' poetry is centered upon real human experience, actual responses to this experience, and
true human efforts to cope with the feelings and
thoughts human life provokes.

Authentic religion does not begin with doctrines
or history or any external authority. Religion becomes
an insight to human experience when that experience admits to no other ultimate understanding. Robinson, and
many readers of Hopkins like him, simply does not penetrate the phenomenology of religious experience which is
expressed in Hopkins' writing. Failure to achieve such
insights forces such readers to construct in Hopkins'
work an essentially false paradigm of religion. The
basic flaw in such thinking is the assumption that faith

is a set of doctrines which must be rationalized upon
personal experience and, if successful, such doctrinal
positions will be "interiorized," that is, somehow these
truths will bring about some felt reconciliation between
one's choices and desires. This is a form of Christian
Rationalism which has abounded even in the Church itself.

But Hopkins' life and art are not rationalizations
of Christian faith; they are authenticating religious
explorations of the core of human experience. And what
is turned up by such exploration? First, the real human
condition is one of being trapped in this place and this
time with insufferable bounds on one's ability to
escape life's circumstances. Time is a rope about one's
neck, the body is a weight around one's spirit, and
death a chain about one's heart. We are encumbered.
The second awareness that turns up is that this earth
must not be our home, for nothing is clearer to the human
consciousness than the human truth that we feel this
life to be fundamentally a dislocation from some place
where we would be truly at home. Human beings therefore are in some basic existential way alien to their
current earthly existence. As one lives, a thousand
little circumstances add up to this state of consciousness. Hopkins' early poetry traces out this "little
sickness in the air" in poem after poem.

Pain of a deep spiritual kind is the result of being jailed in this life's prison house. How does one
deal with the resulting feelings of failed expectations, discouragement, even despair? In his poetry,
Hopkins talks about these feelings a great deal. It is
in this sphere that religious experience has its origin.
The heart seeks consolation for and the head some explanation of the human dilemma. In Hopkins' case, as
his writings make abundantly clear, such emotional dis-
turbances are taken as the "objective correlatives" for
the religious meanings of Christianity. The Christian
account of Creation, Original Sin, and the Incarnation,
as learned dogmas merely words and notions, become
grounded in actual experiences of human restlessness
and attached to real feelings of discontent. What began
as faith, a kind of memorized theory in the head, becomes religion, a felt awareness actively incorporated
in personal experience, sometimes terrifying and always
disconcerting, of realizing the lostness of just being
one solitary person held up only by "Selfyeast." Christianity now becomes deeply personalized by becoming a
disposition in the consciousness by and through which to

deal with the distraught feelings of emptiness, nonful-
fillment, meaninglessness. Now there arises in the human breast a hopeful account of human life which con-
fronts the traps of life; now there is a basis upon
which to encounter this earth, this life, in positive
ways; existence can be consolingly construed as instru-
ments to something else, mysterious albeit, but some
tendered ultimate resolution freely proffered by some
higher being and freely accepted in trust. The trite
phrase is "gift of faith," but it is a real disposition
of spirit.

Out of this emerging, joyous resolution comes the
beginnings of personal triumph. Hopkins' poetry through
and through is a poetry of personal, religious triumph.
In his writings, Hopkins celebrates his great Christian
discovery, for which he coined his now famous terms,
"inscape" and "instress," that God *is* present in the
world in every thing and every person through Christ,
"the first outstress of God's power." Now the primary
duty of this life is clear: "...tho' he is under the
world's splendour and wonder,/His mystery must be instressed, stressed...." The way to encounter the
world's sorrow is to penetrate our natural experiences
to the level of the "inscape" of Christ in its deep
form by means of a consciousness disposed to love, to
trust, to seek goodness, and to find joy. The resulting spiritual transformation will be a more intense appreciation of the mortal beauties of this life, now and
then a glimpse of the "Christ-scape" at play in things,
and a thrilling presentiment of the immortal freedom
beyond this life seen in the "instress" of the wonderful
achievements of natural being: "My heart in hiding/
Stirred for a bird,--the achieve of, the mastery of the
thing!" Most of Hopkins' main body of poetry is poetry
of this kind of celebratory triumph of Christian spirituality, singing to us of God's mastery of the world,
and of His mysterious mastering of the human race. His
poetry is a poetry of religious experience in which the
poet locates his religious feelings and faith in his
senses, in his exploring consciousness, in his "inscaping" words. Hopkins authenticates and validates
Christ playing "in ten thousand places" in his own
experiences of himself experiencing life in the real
world. His emphasis upon locating Christ in general human experience is what makes Hopkins a different kind
of religious poet, a new kind of Christian poet. It is
his Christian empiricism that makes him unique in the
annals of religious poetry, an essential and distin-
guishing quality of his writing which those of his own

persuasion did not understand (and still don't for the most part) and those outside find "fanciful" (one of the forms of consoling euphoria): "(And here the faithful waver, the faithless fable and miss)." Robinson dubs this quality in Hopkins *Romantic* and he is right, for Hopkins should be placed in the highest mode of Romantic consciousness; he is the purest Romantic author in this cultural movement. No other Romantic, English or Continental, achieved more consistently in his writing the spiritual idealism of the Romantic consciousness. His poetry was produced out of a religious intensity of imaginative inspiration not matched by any poet since Blake.

So, however, one is plunged into life's passion, it is a high Romantic's faith that there are natural human releases which will begin to offer relief, encourage one's talent, start to fill human emptiness, intimate that this life is but a birthing. Nature and personality will not remove the nets of our trap; they can begin to untie the knot allowing us to see beyond to ultimate rejuvenation and communion. In Hopkins' writing this emancipation comes down to being open to beauty of all kinds and in that openness, that willingness to see clearly and hold dearly, will come consolation and hope. Lines and lines of his poetry say how beauty "keeps warm men's wits to the things that are...." But there is another insight threaded all throughout Hopkins' poetry. Over and over again he notes that all spiritualizing consciousness depends upon some help from God--"God's better beauty, grace." The human means to grace is an ever deeper "instress" of Christ in one's life. Out of this identification, out of steadfast perseverance through a properly disposed spiritual consciousness, will come those Divine aids which will affirm, encourage, console one's life and fill it with joy. This is the process of Christian sanctification.

Grace, however, does not always come in such positive ways. Sometimes God seems to send His gifts through negative experiences. For example, the religious personality will ill-dispose itself to receive grace thereby installing a great need of the awareness of the need for God's support, or sometimes the religious consciousness becomes overcome by disappointment, depressed by frustrations, wearied by physical illness, discontent with one's station and duty in life, or even feels abandoned by God's care and concern. Affirmation and hope weaken, sometimes to the point of desolation. These moments of spiritual draught, so in striking

38

contrast to those wonderful moments of affirming and uplifting grace, seem not to be moments of grace at all, but rather punishments and chastisements for being human, for failing, for being one's self. Yet these are moments of grace, but moments in which it takes great spiritual courage to suffer depression, to continue to reach out for help, to be patient until these dark graces turn in the mysteriousness of God's will to light. Though Hopkins did not write as many poems on this aspect of Christian spirituality, the few that he did write are among the most telling and powerful in all religious poetry. How hard it is to renew one's sense of God's power and presence in this purgative way! Yet the purity of soul that emerges clearly makes one more worthy to obtain a closer union with God, and through such individual sanctification a greater communion with all mankind. In his poetry of this period Hopkins shows, however difficult it is that divine purpose is realized only in a partnership of mutual mercy and kindness and love. Then will come "in a flash, at a trumpet crash...immortal diamond," as Christ promised.

These sketches are but the outlines of the Christian, religious consciousness in Hopkins' life and writing; they reveal the chief characteristics, however. The pattern of his religious experiences is at once profoundly human, giving them universal identification and general human sympathy, and at the same time they are uniquely individual, giving them distinctive flavors and special qualities. While his spirituality is basically Christian and Catholic and specifically Ignatian, what pours through his writing is the pervading humanness of his religious mentality. His poetry tells us with great dramatic intensity, loving tenderness, and suffering courage what it is like to love and serve God with one's whole mind and heart and being. Because his writing captures the drama of real religious experience, Hopkins has readers who value spiritual life of a very different character from his own. These readers find the religious experience expressed in his writings valid responses to human life, truly religious in feeling, and deeply relevant to the human spiritual process. Hopkins speaks to any person who feels life's yoke and yearns for it to be lifted. Out of this fluttering hope begins the soul's spiritual journey into the mystery of religious experience.

However, those who approach Hopkins from a strictly literary or intellectual tradition may miss the direct simplicity of the religious experience in his writing.

This is especially true for readers whose imaginative perimeters are secular; the religious and theological implications of Hopkins' writing remain largely vague, obscure, or totally unrecognizable. This is why such readers as critics spend the most time talking about the ambiguities in the poet's personality, irregularities in his artistic thinking and practice, and generally the kinds of subjective responses one might have to such "naive" poetry. But to these readers as well, Hopkins speaks directly and forthrightly about life's cage and conflicts, the uses of this life, and the heartburn of unfulfilled destiny. He holds us all with the "glittering eye" of his poetic "inscapes."

Biographers of Hopkins will have to plumb the character of Hopkins' deep and abiding personal spirituality; they should trace in some detail the pattern of his religious experience both as revealed in his prose writings and particularly as it is revealed in his poetry. Attention must be paid to the theological underpinnings of his religious experience in sorting out the traditional from the individual aspects. Surely no biography that might be called "definitive" can fail to address the question of Hopkins' religious experience, the spiritual process of his consciousness, and the true character of his religious imagination. Sanctity is God's business but sanctification is partly a human journey.

In re-reading my own biographical essay written over twenty years ago, I am surprised that in the ensuing time so little has turned up which might change its accuracy and nothing which would force a radical alteration of its point of view. True we have a more detailed understanding of Hopkins' Jesuit life that was not available to me, more family letters, and perhaps a better grasp of the Hopkins family; Hopkins scholarship has sharpened biographical perspective on parts of Hopkins' life. It may be asked, do we not have a "definitive" biography, though in parts, done by different hands, still a composite of Hopkins as good as we will ever get?

The two most recent biographies answer the question. The life of Gerard Manley Hopkins is yet to be written which captures the essence of the man, the genius of his talent, and the splendor of his holiness.[56] All of us who revere Hopkins need and want a true biographical portrait. Soon it will be a century since Hopkins died and still no "work that wakes."

Maybe one will be produced which will still these re-
grets. Meantime we must abide this dark grace and remember Hopkins' own reflection upon such creative ab-
sences: "PATIENCE, hard thing!/the hard thing to pray,/
But bid for, Patience is!"

NOTES

1. See Pierre Pourrat, *Christian Spirituality* (Westminster, Maryland, 1955), IV, 449.

2. *The Letters of Gerard Manley Hopkins to Robert
Bridges*, ed. by C. C. Abbott (London, 1935), p. 225.
Hereafter cited as *Letters to Bridges*.

3. John H. Newman, *Apologia pro Vita sua: being a
History of His Religious Opinions*, ed. by Charles F.
Harrold (New York, 1947), p. 209.

4. G. F. Lahey, S.J., *Gerard Manley Hopkins* (London,
1930), pp. 52-53.

5. *Ibid.*, p. 66.

6. *Letters to Bridges*, pp. 5-6.

7. *Ibid.*, p. 22.

8. *Further Letters of Gerard Manley Hopkins including
his Correspondence with Coventry Patmore*, ed. by C. C.
Abbott (London, 1938), p. 261. Hereafter cited as
Further Letters.

9. *Ibid.*, p. 84.

10. *The Spiritual Exercises of St. Ignatius Loyola*,
tr. by John Morris, S.J. (Westminster, Maryland, 1943),
p. 3.

11. Eleanor Ruggles, *Gerard Manley Hopkins* (New York,
1944), p. 92.

12. I. A. Richards, *Practical Criticism* (New York,
1929), p. 9.

13. I. A. Richards, *Principles of Literary Criticism*
(New York, 1955), p. 265.

14. I. A. Richards, "Gerard Hopkins," *The Dial*, Sept. 19, 1926, 195-206. There are well over twenty published interpretations of this sonnet, and many of them show Mr. Richards' influence.

15. Herbert Read, "Poetry and Belief in Gerard Manley Hopkins," *New Verse* No. 1 (Jan., 1933); also "The Poetry of Gerard Manley Hopkins," *English Critical Essays, Twentieth Century* (London, 1933), pp. 351-74.

16. Lahey, *op. cit.*, pp. 140-43.

17. Ruggles, *op. cit.*, p. 286.

18. Austin Warren, "Gerard Manley Hopkins," *Kenyon Critics* (Norfolk, Connecticut, 1945), p. 14.

19. *Further Letters*, p. 9.

20. *The Correspondence of Gerard Manley Hopkins and Richard Watson Dixon*, ed. C. C. Abbott (London, 1935), p. 93.

21. The phrase, "great sacrifice," appears again and again in Hopkins' spiritual writings, an expression with which he designated a kind of triple heroism in Christ: creaturehood, incarnation, and crucifixion.

22. *Sermons and Devotional Writings*, ed. by C. Devlin, S.J. (London, 1959), pp. 253-54. Hereafter referred to as *Spiritual Writings*.

23. *Ibid.*

24. Arthur Mizener, "Victorian Hopkins," *Kenyon Critics* (Norfolk, Connecticut, 1945), p. 98.

25. *Ibid.*, p. 103.

26. *Ibid.*, p. 113.

27. This may have been an influence in Hopkins' not being permitted an additional year of theological study, thus shutting off the possibility of a professorship of theology in the Society.

28. *Spiritual Writings*, p. 119.

29. *Poems of Gerard Manley Hopkins*, ed. W. H. Gardner (London, 1948), p. xxi.

30. John Pick, *Gerard Manley Hopkins* (London, 1942), pp. 25-6.

31. See D. A. Downes, *Gerard Manley Hopkins: A Study of His Ignatian Spirit* (New York, 1959), Ch. Five, especially pp. 130-36.

32. See a forthright presentation and discussion in Louis Bouyer's *Newman: His Life and Spirituality*, tr. by J. Lewis May (New York, 1959); also an excellent particular example in Vincent F. Blehl, "Newman and the Missing Miter," *Thought*, XXXV (1960), 111-23.

33. Bernard Bergonzi, *Gerard Manley Hopkins* (New York: Collier Masters of World Literature Series, Macmillan, 1977).

34. Paddy Kitchen, *Gerard Manley Hopkins* (London: Hamish Hamilton, 1978; New York: Atheneum, 1979).

35. Alfred Thomas, S.J., *Hopkins the Jesuit: The Years of Training* (London: Oxford University Press, 1968).

36. Alison G. Sulloway, *Gerard Manley Hopkins and the Victorian Temper* (New York: Columbia University Press, 1972; London: Routledge & Kegan Paul, 1972).

37. Michael Allsopp, S.J., "Hopkins at Highgate: Biographical Fragments," *The Hopkins Quarterly*, VI, No. 1 (Spring, 1979), 3-11; "Hopkins at Oxford, 1863-1867: His Formal Studies," *The Hopkins Quarterly*, IV, Nos. 3 & 4 (Fall & Winter, 1977-1978), 161-177. Also of interest see Patricia L. Skarda, "Juvenalia of the Family of Gerard Manley Hopkins," *The Hopkins Quarterly*, IV, No. 12 (Summer, 1977), 39-55.

38. Francis Keegan, S.J., "Gerard Manley Hopkins at Mount St. Mary's College Spinkhill, 1847-1878," *The Hopkins Quarterly*, VI, No. 1 (Spring, 1979), 11-35; Gerald Roberts, "The Jaded Muse: Hopkins at Stonyhurst," *The Hopkins Quarterly*, VI, No. 1 (Spring, 1979), 35-47.

39. *All My Eyes See: The Visual World of Gerard Manley Hopkins*, R. K. R. Thornton, ed. (Sunderland: Geolfrith Press and Sunderland Arts Council, 1975).

40. Jean-George Ritz, *Robert Bridges and Gerard Manley Hopkins (1863-1889): A Literary Friendship* (London: Oxford University Press, 1960).

41. See Elisabeth W. Schneider, *The Dragon in the Gate: Studies in the Poetry of G. M. Hopkins* (Berkeley: University of California Press, 1968), pp. 135-39.

42. Donald E. Stafford, *In the Classic Mode: The Achievement of Robert Bridges* (Newark: University of Delaware Press, 1978).

43. David A. Downes, *Victorian Portraits: Hopkins and Pater* (New York: Bookman Associates, Inc., 1965).

44. John Robinson, *In Extremity: A Study of Gerard Manley Hopkins* (London: Cambridge University Press, 1978).

45. See Wendell Stacy Johnson, "Sexuality and Inscape," *The Hopkins Quarterly*, III, No. 2 (July, 1876), 59-66; Michael Lynch, "Recovering Hopkins, Recovering Ourselves," *The Hopkins Quarterly*, VI, No. 36 (Fall, 1979), 107-18.

46. Robinson, p. 95.

47. F. X. Shea, S.J., "Religion and the Romantic Movement," *Studies in Romanticism*, IX (Fall, 1970), 293-96.

48. *Poems of Gerard Manley Hopkins*, ed. with additional notes, a foreword revised text, and a new biographical and critical introduction by W. H. Gardner and N. H. MacKenzie (4th ed., Oxford University Press, 1967), pp. 86, 99, 103.

49. *Ibid.*, p. 107.

50. *Ibid.*, pp. 76, 90.

51. Robinson, p. 91.

52. *Ibid.*, p. 92.

53. *Ibid.*, pp. 83-99.

54. *Ibid.*, pp. 82-104.

55. *Ibid.*, pp. 91-92.

56. In 1977 a special seminar on Hopkins' biography was held at the annual convention of the Modern Language Association. The papers read were published in *The*

Hopkins Quarterly, IV, Nos. 3 & 4 (Fall & Winter, 1977-78). The status of Hopkins' biography was then revealed as follows: Anthony Bischoff, S.J., was at that time still at work on his full biography and also a Mr. Bevis Hillier was also at work on a complete biography. The current information was that both writers would soon publish "definitive" biographies. Now four years later, we are still waiting for both the British and American versions. How wonderful it would be to have one or both on or before the centenary of Hopkins' birth. Indeed we may have three. The International Hopkins Association (Summer, 1982) announces that Norman White of University College, Dublin, is completing a sabbatical year during which he has been preparing a biography of Hopkins to be published by Oxford University Press.

THE COUNTERPOISE IN G. M. HOPKINS

In an exchange of letters during November and December, 1881, R. W. Dixon and G. M. Hopkins discussed
poetry and the priesthood. Dixon said, "Surely one vocation cannot destroy another: and such a Society as
yours will not remain ignorant that you have such gifts
as have seldom been given by God to man."[1] Hopkins responded with a long explanation of his notion of "God's
service" and his views on the Jesuits and culture.
Pointing out that the Society has sometimes contributed
to culture in its service to God, he noted, "...that
literature proper, as poetry, has seldom been found to be
to that end a very serviceable means...there have been
very few Jesuit poets and, where they have been, I believe it would be found on examination that there was
something exceptional in their circumstances, or, so to
say, counterbalancing in their career."[2] Here Hopkins
launched into a survey of Jesuits who attained distinction of one sort or another. In each instance, he
pointed out counterbalancing elements in their lives
which neutralized the dangers of individual fame: "In
England we had Fr. Southwell a poet, a minor poet but
still a poet: but he wrote amidst a terrible persecution
and died a martyr, with circumstances of horrible bar-
barity: this is the counterpoise in his career."[3]

While there is no rancor in his letter, more a
quelling of Dixon's astonishment, the explanation offered describes the precarious predicament of Hopkins'
poetic genius. What he really was telling the Anglican
Canon was that he had as yet no "counterpoise" in his
career which would give him justification to write less
spasmodically and even publish occasionally. I do not
mean to suggest that Hopkins was looking for an excuse.
What he did want very much was to make something of his
priesthood, both professionally and spiritually. A
good and God-fearing man, Dixon was amazed and saddened
that Hopkins seemed to think that his poetry was very
much of an aside to his praising and serving God. And
so has been most everyone since. Nevertheless, Hopkins
believed what he wrote. How he lived it is his story,
the search for a "counterpoise" for his muse.

II

A priest-poet needed a "counterpoise," Hopkins
dimly perceived when he decided to take holy orders: "I

47

want to write still and as a priest I very likely can do
that too, not so freely as I should have liked, e.g.
nothing or little in the verse way, but no doubt what
would best serve the cause of my religion."[4] He calmly
affirmed harmony between his two vocations. To be sure,
the priesthood was to take the lead, but he hoped that
the "Jesuit Discipline"[5] would not be too hard on the
poet. He probably "burned" his poetry with equanimity
when he entered the Jesuit order.[6]

Even in 1875, there was no cause for anxiety over
poetry. His superior had expressed the wish for a poem
on the *Deutschland* wreck, and Hopkins responded with a
long, ornate ode full of the sound and fury of stormy
salvation.[7] With his ordination in 1877, the prospects
of a more substantial "counterpoise" than a hint of a
superior was in the offing. While the missions were un-
likely, the pursuit of theology (and implicitly in the
Scholastic tradition, philosophy) was.

While at Oxford, Hopkins had shown enough interest
in philosophy to formulate a theory of ideogenesis as
his essays on words and Parmenides show.[8] Already in
1868, he had begun developing his notion of "inscape,"
"stressing," and "instress." So it was quite natural
that when he began his philosophy as a Jesuit, he picked
up where he left off. But in doing the first course,
psychology, he received little inspiration, for he was
taught the rational psychology of Francisco Suarez (a
sixteenth-century Jesuit theologian who attempted to
amalgamate the various Scholastic trends into one main
system) who emphasized the Aristotelian-Aquinian episte-
mological tradition rather than the Platonic-Augustinian.
Put overly simply, this meant that Hopkins was probably
taught that all human knowledge is obtained only through
the senses, thus eliminating the theory of innate knowledge.

Hopkins was disenchanted when he finished his
course in 1871.[9] Suarez was of no avail to his speculations. Surely, in the Scholastic tradition, there
must be one whose perspectives would be more accommo-
dating to his own theories, while still being a rather
complete, equally compelling, fully orthodox thinker.
His *Notebook* records for August 3, 1872: "At this time
I had first begun to get hold of the copy of Scotus on
the Sentences in the Baddely library and was flush with
a new stroke of enthusiasm. It may come to nothing or
it may be a mercy from God. But just then when I took
in any inscape of the sky or sea I thought of Scotus."[10]

It came to nothing as the "counterpoise" he was
seeking. Hopkinsians will not like this, and they will
point to the interesting esthetic and theological speculation which Scotus occasioned in Hopkins.[11] I am of
no mind to deny a certain brilliance to Hopkins' theological speculation nor an engaging sketch of a theory
of esthetics. Even the little of both he left in his
writings indicates the originality and range of his
mind. Still, after his ordination, his Jesuit preceptors denied him a further year of theological studies
which would have set him on a path to a professorship
in theology or scripture. He might have had his "counterpoise." Looking back, he seemed to offer considerable promise. The historian of University College,
Dublin, remembered the promise and the difficulty:
"...as a theologian his undoubted brilliance was dimmed
by a somewhat obstinate love of Scotist doctrine, in
which he traced the influence of Platonist philosophy.
His idiosyncrasy got him into difficulty with his
Jesuit preceptors...."[12]

III

     Preaching the word of God is one of the prime
duties of holy orders. It would most certainly qualify
as a licit means of employing talent. Hopkins began
his career at the famous London church known as "Farm
Street" with a series of three sermons in August of
1878. As his letters to Bridges indicate, he was most
confident and eager. In November he was moved to Oxford to serve the parish church of St. Aloysius. The
move seemed hopeful, for there was the possibility that
he might have become a sort of chaplain to the Catholics
in the University, a post where his talents and experience could have been beneficial.

     Within a year, Hopkins was dispatched again. His
year at Oxford was a disappointment. He seemed indis-
posed to serve either the Town or the Gown. He did not
have a thriving relationship with his superior, Fr. T.
B. Parkinson, who kept University relationships in his
own hands. At a suggestion of a colleague, Fr. William
Humphrey, Hopkins began writing out his sermons. We
have six from his last three months at Oxford. While
some are brilliant with rhetorical effect, they lack
what Hopkins himself was to call *bidding*, "the art or
virtue of saying everything right *to* or *at* the hearer,
interesting him, holding him."[13]

His next assignment was a big parish church in
Liverpool, St. Francis Xavier's. But before taking up
residence in Liverpool, he was to put in three months
at Bedford Leigh, a small industrial town near Manches-
ter. Here he seems to have found himself as a preacher,
perhaps, because he felt for the first time the shep-
herdry of the priesthood. Whatever, his letters and
sermons ebb and flow in the full tide of "bidding." He
told his friend, Baillie: "Oxford was not to me a con-
genial field, fond as I am of it; I am more at home with
the Lancashire people."[14]

The Bedford Leigh sermons are filled with homey
words of simple piety. They were a modest success and
more than likely, Hopkins went on to Liverpool with
something of a preaching reputation. At least when he
arrived, he was immediately assigned to give a course of
four Sunday evening sermons in a pulpit regularly occu-
pied by distinguished preachers who spoke to very large
crowds. Here was a first rate opportunity to establish
a true reputation.

He began satisfactorily with a sermon on the theme,
"Duty is Love." Its directness and simplicity were
promising. In the second of the series, he launched
into the first of a trilogy on "The Kingdom of God."
Hopkins had some original notions on this subject, aided
and abetted by Scotus (whom he had been reading since
1872). He announced his plan: "...tonight therefore
let our thoughts be turned to God's kingdom as it was
first founded upon earth and next Sunday we shall, I
hope, see its history, its glory, and its fall."[15]

In order to put across this recondite theological
subject, Hopkins resorted to political idiom: "God is
our king." He skillfully drew his version of the compact
of *original justice* (immunity from sin and concupis-
cence); he ended by announcing: "And all fell, all is
gone...." Now, with the grandiosity of this matter, his
full powers were being called into action, not only his
expressive ability, but also his creativity. His superior may have discerned that his parish was in for some
original theological speculation, and his new man did
not waylay these feelings in his next sermon.

A week later Hopkins examined in detail the terms
of God's compact with man and the consequences of its
breaching. He overran his time, and again he ended on
the note of the dissolution of God's kingdom. Whether
the Rector of the parish, Fr. James Clare, understood

the original blend of Aquinas and Scotus that Hopkins
was expressing, I do not know. A fine preacher himself,
he may very well have become disturbed with the young
priest's sense of dialectic. Twice Hopkins had ended on
very negative notes, and then he entitled his next effort, "on the Fall of God's First Kingdom." It was too
much as the note Hopkins wrote over the text sadly records: "I was not allowed to take this title and on the
printed bills it was covered by a blank slip pasted
over. The text too I changed to last week's, and had
to leave out or reword all passages speaking of God's
kingdom as falling."[17] This undoubtedly hurt the young
curate, for two years later he returned to this climactic sermon and wrote a long explanatory note. It suggests his curtailment was something more than bad
preaching strategy.

For three months he was not called on to preach.
Then he was named again to preach the Sunday gospel of
April 25, but a note appended to the sermon indicates
discouragement: "Notes (for it seems that written sermons do no good)."[18] The sermon is a brilliant example
of his exegetical ability. He was called on again for
Sunday, May 30. Again, he wrote a fine exegesis of the
parable of the supper and the guests who would not come,
but it was not given. A visitor took his place. This
happened again on June 29, 1880. He remained fifteen
months more at Liverpool and was asked to preach only
three more Sunday sermons. One of these is a great
sermon,[19] a combination of spiritual insight and verbal
eloquence which was beyond the capacities of his lis-
teners.

But the disappointments were welling up. He
preached on short notice one of his sermons from Bedford
Leigh.[20] At first he was pleased, for he seemed to have
moved some of his hearers to tears, but when he preached
a week later, he noted drearily, "...but when the thing
happened next week I perceived that it was hot and that
it was sweat they were wiping away."[21] Whether they
were or not, there is little question about Hopkins'
disappointment. On October 25, 1880, he preached on
"Divine Providence and the Guardian Angels." The fourth
line of the sermon reads, "He [God] takes more interest
in a merchant's business than the merchant, in a ves-
sel's steering than the pilot, in a lover's sweetheart
than the lover, in a sick man's pain than the sufferer,
in our salvation than we ourselves." The line is bro-
ken with a crushing note: "[In consequence of this word
sweetheart I was in a manner suspended and at all events

was forbidden (it was some time after) to preach without having my sermon revised. However, when I was going to take the next sermon I had to give after this regulation came into force to Fr. Clare for revision he poohpoohed the matter and would not look at it.]"[22] There are three more extant sermons, and Hopkins tells he preached more that he did not write down. However, the record of his disillusion is clear.

When he was assigned to Liverpool, Hopkins surmised he was in for a trying time. His letters document the unfortunate fulfillment. His first letter to Dixon from Liverpool answers the Canon's request for more of Hopkins' poetry: "The parish work of Liverpool is very wearing to mind and body and leaves me nothing but odds and ends of time."[23] This was May 14. Two weeks before, he told his mother of his illness during the Easter season when work is the heaviest: "Neither am I very strong now and as long as I am in Liverpool I do not see how I can be; not that I complain of this, but I state it."[24] He told his friend Baillie, on May 22: "At least I can say my Liverpool work is very harrassing and makes it hard to write."[25]

By September, he was caving in both physically and spiritually. He opened his letter to Bridges on September 5: "I take up a languid pen to write you, being down with diarrhea and vomiting, brought on by yesterday's heat and the long hours in the confessional."[26] Again in October: "I daresay you have long deserved an answer...But I never could write; time and spirits were wanting; one is so fagged, so harried and galled up and down. And the drunkards go on drinking, the filthy, as the scripture says, are filthy still: human nature is so inveterate. Would that I had seen the last of it."[27] And he still had almost a full year to go! But he wearied his way through.

Hopkins was assigned to begin his third year of noviceship (tertianship) before taking his final vows on October 10, 1881. He was to go back where he had begun it all, Manresa House, Roehampton, and he welcomed the change and the chance to survey the damage: "...I feel that I need the noviceship very much and shall be every way better off when I have been made more spiritual minded."[28] As we shall see, he did recoup enough to begin all over.

As for his preaching, it would be unfair to say that Hopkins was decidedly a failure. Reading his

sermons, one is often struck by their fresh theological
perspectives, the courage to attack difficult sermon
topics, and a frequent brilliance and beauty of composition. And the spiritual value afforded to those who
heard them, we shall never know. His short stature and
high-pitched voice certainly were handicaps when coupled
with his chronic inability to estimate his congrega-
tions--and his superiors! Professionally speaking
though, Fr. Clare's "poohpoohing" is the keynote to this
"counterpoise" in G. M. Hopkins.

IV

The year of tertianship (1881-82) proved, as Hopkins
had hoped it would, to be a period of regeneration. He
began it very hopefully. After explaining to Dixon that
tertianship is a second noviceship in preparation for
taking last vows and asserting his fidelity to his vocation, he commented: "Besides all which, my mind is here
more at peace than it has ever been and I would gladly
live all my life, if it were to be, in as great or a
greater seclusion from the world and be busied only with
God."[29] His first letter to Bridges from Roehampton is
filled with new fervor and buoyancy: "This spot, though
it has suffered much from decay of nature and more from
the hand of man, is still beautiful. It is besides a
great rest to be here and I am in a very contented frame
of mind."[30]

It proved to be a wonderfully creative year. Hopkins composed the bulk of his spiritual writing during
this year (nearly a hundred printed pages) and laid
down plans for five different works: a commentary on the
Spiritual Exercises (which he began during a month's
meditation on them), a study of sacrifice in ancient
religions, a treatise on the lyric art of Greece, an
ode on Edmund Campion, and a drama based on the life of
St. Winefred. So he had projected three works in prose
and two in verse. If not as a theologian or a preacher,
then he might find his counterbalance as a scholar
(sometimes writer), an endeavor highly suitable to his
talents.

It is not relevant here to examine the many insights and comments he made on the *Spiritual Exercises*
during his second noviceship.[31] However, there are two
aspects of his spiritual writings which bear on Hopkins'
"counterpoise." One is his ever-deepening conviction
of the kind of "counterpoise" that there must be in his

53

life. His inspiration here was the life of Christ. He
called it "the great sacrifice" of Christ. It was based
on St. Paul's epistle to the Philippians (ii, 5-11). In
sum it was that Christ performed three great acts of
sacrifice by making Himself subservient to His Father,
to the angels and to men: "...he emptied or exhausted
himself so far as that was possible, of godhead and behaved only as God's slave, as his creature, as man,
which he also was, and then being in the guise of man
humbled himself to death, the death of the cross." He
had a light on how the Incarnation shaped the lives of
men: "It is this holding of himself back, and not
snatching at the truest and highest good, the good that
was his right, nay his possession from a past eternity
in his other nature, his own being and self, which seems
to me the root of all his holiness and the imitation of
this the root of all moral good in men."32 The "counterpoise" must be determined by Christ.

The other note is equally important. It might be
called "personality and the counterpoise." Victorianism
itself called for a kind of counterbalance in life, and
I offer the opinion that the greatest evidence of this
lies in the religious sensibility of that day which asserted an inevitable strife between personality and
goodness. I think that this is nowhere more evident
in the life of a Victorian than it is in Hopkins' life.
One would have expected Hopkins to have been duly influenced as a Jesuit by the great emphasis St. Ignatius
puts upon the notion that true charity lies in the union
of duty and desire, or integrated personality. The
whole design of the *Spiritual Exercises* is to achieve
this end. St. Ignatius' famous letters on obedience offer counsels on obtaining this state within the Society
of Jesus.

Moreover, Scotus, Hopkins' "rarest-veined unravel-
ler," stressed, contrary to the Victorian code, that
desire and choice should go together. If there is inevitable opposition between the two, human personality
is normally traumatically bifurcated, and man's psychic
state is thus perpetually anxious, and in a state of
deep, internal conflict. But this is not normal personality, and all of Hopkins' spiritual guides told him
so.

Though there is good reason to believe that Hopkins
knew this, still in his writings on human personality
he says that human nature and personality are arbitrarily joined.33 So it follows that there can be no

54

natural impulse to goodness or God, for all impetus must come from an act of choice or through the "elective will." Duty then is a struggle against our nature to do that which is either repugnant or indifferent to our "affective" selves. Why Hopkins should have continued to exaggerate the distinction between our "elective" and "affective" selves, I do not know, but it does amount to a kind of adjustment of the Ignatian view of personality to that of Victorian Protestantism. As we shall see, this view of personality coupled with the "great sacrifice" was in the time of crisis to show the way to spiritual heroism and tragedy.

V

After Hopkins made his Last Vows, he was appointed to teach classics at Stonyhurst: "My appointment is to teach our 'philosophers' (like undergraduate students) Latin, Greek, and perhaps hereafter English (when I know more about it) for the London B.A. degree."[34] The time certainly seemed propitious for some serious writing, for Hopkins was now in happy circumstances as his letters show. The only question was the approval of his Provincial (superior for all English Jesuits). Apparently, Hopkins outlined some of his interests to his superior, and while he did not receive strong encouragement, he was not prohibited. He reported his interview to Bridges: "The Provincial further added that what time was left over I might employ in writing one or other of the books I had named to him. But very little time will be left over and I cd. never make time."[35] But could he get anything done if there was time? He closed the paragraph quoted above with a worry: "Indeed now, with nothing to do but prepare, I cannot get forward with my ode. But one must hope against hope."

There was time in fact, and Hopkins was making some use of it. By early October he had finished the choruses for St. Winefred's Well. Apparently he had Beuno's speech by December. Yet something was wrong. He told his dear friend Baillie: "I am here to coach classics.... I like my pupils and do not wholly dislike the work, but I fall into or continue in a heavy, weary state of body and mind.... I make no way with what I read, and seem but half a man."[36] He told Bridges in March the same and by June, Dixon had heard.

The listlessness and ennui continued until the autumn of 1883. Even his meeting with Coventry Patmore

on 29 July 1883 (when Patmore was on a visit to Stonyhurst) did not spark Hopkins. It is true that they
struck off a warm friendship: they exchanged letters,
and Hopkins assisted Patmore with a new edition of his
Poems by offering a considerable number of suggestions
and evaluations. Hopkins visited briefly with Patmore
at his home in Hastings during August, 1885. Whatever
impetus there might have been, it fell far short, perhaps because of what had transpired when he made his retreat at Beaumont, September, 1883.

Hopkins jotted down a page and a half of private
notes he made during his retreat, but their brevity, in
my opinion, belies their importance. First, in meditating on his sins, he became so upset that he was ad-
vised (a suggestion that was frequent) to leave off
considering them. While there is some question whether
Hopkins was scrupulous, there is no question that his
conscience was a hard taskmaster. Second, he considered
his religious performance cowardly and had to settle for
trying to perform well his ordinary duties. Third,
"During this retreat I have much and earnestly prayed
that God will lift me above myself to a higher state of
grace, in which I may have more union with him, be more
zealous to do his will, and freer from sin."

But how was this to be done through services ren-
dered? He had failed to make any significant contribution to the Society either as a theologian or preacher.
It now seemed that nothing was to come of his professional writing. As he himself said, "...I do little in
the way of hard penances...." He could perform his ordinary duties well, for he had been assured this was a
"great part of life" of the holiest men. Surely though,
there was something more he could do, some little
sacrifice not unworthy of the "great sacrifice." Was
there a "counterpoise" for him?

There was only one thing he could do: "Also in
some med. today I earnestly asked our Lord to watch
over my compositions, not to preserve them from being
lost or coming to nothing, for that I am very willing
they should be, but they might not do me harm through
enmity or imprudence of any man or my own; that he
should have them as his own and employ or not employ
them as he should see fit. And this I believe is
heard." This offering, viewed in the light of Hopkins'
own psychology and Ignatian spirituality, must be
taken to mean that he had chosen to detach himself from
his poetry to the point of personal indifference. The

poetry was to be no longer a real concern. In effect, what Hopkins was doing was bringing his desires into line with his choice of closer union with God. It did not mean that he would write no more; it meant that what he had written or would write was left to its own destiny.

But can one give up one's special self like this? The day after Hopkins had had his "great grace," he had another insight: "In meditating on the Crucifixion I saw how my asking to be raised to a higher degree of grace was asking also to be lifted higher on the cross." And the next day: "The walk to Emmaus. This morning in Thanksgiving after mass much bitter thought but also insight in things. And the above meditation was made in a desolate frame of mind; but towards the end I was able to rejoice in the comfort our Lord gave those two men...." More desolation and the loss of comfort would bring him down to cases where "...thoughts against thoughts in groans grind." There would be no carols in his "counterpoise."

VI

The last years of Hopkins' life are such a wrestling for salvation that they are almost a morality play in five acts. They begin with his "exile" to Ireland in 1884: "To seem the stranger lies my lot, my life/Among strangers."[38] His first letter to Bridges from Dublin sets the stage: "I have been warmly welcomed and most kindly treated. But Dublin itself is a joyless place and I think in my heart as smoky as London is: I had fancied it quite different."[39] Six weeks later in a letter to Baillie,[40] physical and mental deterioration was setting in: "The melancholy I have all my life been subject to has become of late years not indeed more intense in its fits but rather more distributed, constant and crippling. One, the lightest but a very inconvenient form of it, is daily anxiety about work to be done, which makes me break off or never finish all that lies outside that work. It is useless to write more on this: when I am at my worst, though my judgment is never affected, my state is much like madness." The closing lines foreshadow the tragic end of the conflict: "I see no ground for thinking I shall ever get over it or succeed in doing anything that is not forced on me to do of any consequence." Thus the Prologue.

The first act (1885) is full of passion and poetry: "To what serves Mortal Beauty?" "...Our evening is over us; our night whelms, whelms/and will end us." "But ah,

57

but O thou terrible, why wouldst thou rude on me/Thy
wring-world right foot rock?" "Comforter, where, where
is your comforting?" "And my lament/is cries countless,
cries like dead letters sent/To dearest him that lives
alas! away." "We hear our hearts grate on themselves:
It kills/To bruise them dearer." "I cast for comfort
I can no more get...."[41]

The next three acts (1886-88) are filled with pro-
saic attrition. They are gradual in movement, their
very pace illustrative of the passing of vitality. Despite moments of critical acumen and periods of calm,
quite ugly shapes of slavery and madness lurk in Hopkins' letters of this period, even suicide. He was being destroyed by his "counterpoise" but believing this
all he had to offer, he desperately clung to his choice.
There is even some sign of his dissatisfaction with
God's justice in the face of his difficult decision. It
never occurred to him that what he was attempting was
as unnatural as a father being indifferent to the fate
of his children. Though the destruction of the spirit
is often latent, its effects silent beneath the surface,
there comes that sudden moment when the harsh, grating
voice of ravage speaks: "All impulse fails me: I can
give myself no sufficient reason for going on. Nothing
comes: I am a eunuch--but it is for the kingdom of
heaven's sake."[42]

Conventionally, the last act of a morality play is
the soul's reckoning. Hopkins' last retreat (January,
1889) before his death serves the convention well. The
place is St. Stanislaus' College, Tullabeg, Ireland.
This was the novitiate of the Irish Province of Jesuits.
His retreat notes[43] (four double sheets of notepapers
closely written on both sides) provide the drama.

The first three days are a ruthless self-examina-
tion of his life: "The question is how I advance the
side I serve on." He considers his public service in
Ireland, the distressing state of Irish politics, and
the questionable patriotism of the Irish Church. The
accusation is strong: "I do not feel then that out-
wardly I do much good, much that I care to do or can
much wish to prosper; and this is a mournful life to
lead."

But did his inner disposition acquit him? The
consideration was wracking: "I was continuing this train
of thought this evening when I began to enter on that
course of loathing and helplessness which I have so

often felt before, which made me feel madness.... I
could therefore do no more than repeat *Justus es,
Domine, et rectum judicium tuum* and the like.... What
is my wretched life? Five wasted years almost have
passed in Ireland. I am ashamed of the little I have
done, of my waste of time, although helplessness and
weakness is such that I could scarcely do otherwise.
And yet the Wise Man warns us against excusing ourselves
in that fashion. I cannot then be excused; but what is
life without aim, without spur without help? All my
undertakings miscarry: I am like a straining eunuch. I
wish then for death: yet if I died now I should die im-
perfect, no master of myself, and that is the worst
failure of all. O my God, look down on me."

The second day: "This morning I made the meditation
on the Three Sins, with nothing to enter but loathing
of my life and a barren submission to God's will." The
third day: "Helpless loathing." The fourth day there
are no notes. On the fifth day, he reconsidered the
Incarnation: "The Incarnation was for my salvation and
that of the world: the work goes on in a great system
and machinery which even drags me on with the collar
round my neck though I could and do neglect my duty in
it. But I say to myself that I am only too willing to
do God's work and help on the knowledge of the Incarnation. But this is not really true: I am not willing
enough for the piece of work assigned me, the only work
I am given to do, though I could do others if they were
given."

But he had done something leading from the Incarnation: "And I thought that the Royal University was to
me what Augustus's enrollment was to St. Joseph: *exiit
sermo a Caesare Augusto etc.*; so the resolution of the
R.U. came to me, inconvenient and painful; and then I
am bound in justice, and paid." He had some spiritual
footing upon which to find equilibrium, and he strained
for his balance: "I hope to bear this in mind."

Relief came the same day though he did not write
it down until the next: "Yesterday I had ever so much
light...and last night...and today...more than I can
easily put down." The light is on the Epiphany. His
editor, Fr. Christopher Devlin, described the entries:
"In these last notes all is juice sucked from the words
of the gospel, nothing is spun from fancy." He also
provided a comment on the moral drama: "They end with
the cliff-face scaled and his mind at one, striding forward with great strides on a high plateau of light; of
light, or rather of bright shadow...."[44]

I think "bright shadow" is the way the drama ends.
It is true that in his last letters, Hopkins is often
in good spirits despite a continual deterioration of his
health.   Indeed, at the onset of his final sickness, a
month before he died, he wrote to his mother: "My sickness falling at the most pressing time of the University
work, there will be the devil to pay.   Only there is no
harm in saying, that gives *me* no trouble but an unlooked
for relief.   At many such a time I have been in a sort
of extremity of mind, now I am the placidest soul in
the world.   And you will see, when I come round, I shall
be the better for this."[45]

But then the darkness was never done.   There is
the appeal in his sonnet of March: "Mine, O thou lord
of life, send my roots rain."   Even more significant is
the last poem he sent to Bridges in April.   Though it
is entitled, "To R. B.," it is really an epitaph to his
muse: "My winter world, that scarcely breathes..."
Twenty-one years before, Hopkins burnt his verse "...as
not belonging to my profession...";[46] he did not realize,
in his religious exuberance, that he had set himself on
fire.   Perhaps he had his "counterpoise" from that moment on.   When he recognized it finally, he too "...
found it an intolerable grief to submit to it,"[47] but
there is also a splendor in his submission.   It is the
dark light of tragedy.   As in all great tragedy, there
is peace of soul after the purgatorial fire has done
its work.

NOTES

1.   *The Correspondence of Gerard Manley Hopkins and
Richard Watson Dixon*, ed. C. C. Abbott (London: Oxford
University Press, 1935), p. 92.   Hereafter *Letters to
Dixon*.

2.   *Ibid.*, p. 93.

3.   *Ibid.*, p. 94.

4.   *Further Letters of Gerard Manley Hopkins including
his Correspondence with Coventry Patmore*, ed. C. C.
Abbott (London: Oxford University Press, 1956), p. 231.
Hereafter *Further Letters*.

5.   *Ibid.*, p. 408.

6.   *Letters to Dixon*, p. 14.

7. See David A. Downes, *Gerard Manley Hopkins: A Study of His Ignatian Spirit* (New York: Bookman Associates, 1959), pp. 52-73.

8. *The Journals and Papers of Gerard Manley Hopkins*, ed. H. House and G. Storey (London: Oxford University Press, 1959), pp. 125-130. Hereafter *Journals*.

9. Hopkins told Dixon in 1881: "Suarez is our most famous theologian: he is a man of vast volume of mind, but without originality or brilliancy; he treats everything satisfactorily, but you never remember a phrase of his, the manner is nothing." *Letters to Dixon*, p. 95.

10. *Journals*, p. 221.

11. It is not pertinent here to discuss Hopkins and Scotus, but I refer the reader to the introductory essays in the edition of *The Sermons and Devotional Writings of Gerard Manley Hopkins*, ed. Fr. Christopher Devlin, S.J. (London: Oxford University Press, 1959); also his illuminating essays in the *Month*; N.S., III (1950), 114-127, 191-202. Hereafter *Devotional Writings*.

12. *The Letters of Gerard Manley Hopkins to Robert Bridges*, ed. C. C. Abbott (London: Oxford University Press, 1935), p. 319. Hereafter *Letters to Bridges*.

13. *Ibid.*, p. 160.

14. *Further Letters*, p. 243.

15. *Devotional Writings*, p. 54.

16. *Ibid.*, p. 58.

17. *Ibid.*, p. 62.

18. *Ibid.*, p. 68.

19. *Ibid.*, pp. 83-89.

20. *Ibid.*, p. 34.

21. *Ibid.*, p. 81.

22. *Ibid.*, p. 89.

23. *Letters to Dixon*, p. 33.

24. *Further Letters*, p. 157.

25. *Ibid.*, p. 244.

26. *Letters to Bridges*, p. 104.

27. *Ibid.*, p. 110. See also *Letters to Dixon*, p. 42, and *Further Letters*, p. 63.

28. *Ibid.*, p. 135.

29. *Letters to Dixon*, p. 75.

30. *Letters to Bridges*, p. 138.

31. His notes suggest an application of Scotus and more than a little Suarez to Ignatian spirituality. As was usual with Hopkins, his highly individualizing touch is apparent. For his theology, see Fr. Christopher Devlin's essay in *Devotional Writings*, pp. 107-21. For Ignatian spirituality, see Downes, *op. cit.*, pp. 26-51.

32. *Letters to Bridges*, p. 175.

33. *Devotional Writings*, p. 146.

34. *Letters to Bridges*, p. 150.

35. *Ibid.*

36. *Further Letters*, p. 251.

37. *Devotional Writings*, pp. 253-54.

38. *Poems of Gerard Manley Hopkins*, ed. W. H. Gardner (London: Oxford University Press, 1948), p. 109. Hereafter *Poems*.

39. *Letters to Bridges*, p. 190.

40. *Further Letters*, p. 256.

41. *Poems*, pp. 103-11.

42. *Letters to Bridges*, p. 270.

43. *Devotional Writings*, pp. 261-71.

44. *Ibid.*, p. 221.

45. *Further Letters*, p. 197.

46. *Letters to Dixon*, p. 14.

47. *Ibid.*, p. 138.

GRACE AND BEAUTY IN "THE WRECK OF THE DEUTSCHLAND":

A CENTENARY ESTIMATION

"The Wreck of the Deutschland," now a hundred years old, is being accepted in the company of truly great English odes and elegies. This is genuinely astonishing because this has happened against every expectation. The circumstances of its composition and publication, its style, subject matter, and point of view were all false prophets of the poem's future monumentality. In the final assessment, we cannot account for the poem's extraordinary acceptance, for the creative quality of every reader inheres in the poem in a unique way; however, there are reasons to suggest as probable factors in the poem's celebration.

Among the notes supporting popularity in this century is that the work is "high" Victorian--the intrigue of genius wrapped in idiosyncrasy. Besides being written well within the Victorian time-frame, the very circumstances of its genesis are especially appealing to the contemporary serious reader of poetry whose engagement is enhanced if the biography of a poem is fascinating. The fact that this poem was written by a Jesuit religious, that it represented a mysterious sudden shift in poetic sensibility from tyro to professional, that it was an experiment yet it became at the same time a great accomplishment, that it was rooted deeply and richly in personal experience but nevertheless is the expression of the private vision taking on the public stance thereby transforming the personal confessional voice into an oratorical utterance, that it lay hidden in a kind of secret splendor only to be gradually unburied over a long period of time during which its poetic waves have been slowly but with increasing intensity emitting their lovely lights--all of these Victorian aspects of the poem's charisma charm us today. Certainly part of this attraction lies in the twentieth-century attitude that the dreams wherein our contemporary responsibilities began were Victorian dreams. It is as if by re-discovering the past century, we experience a kind of psychogenesis which becomes an enabling act of self-discovery. "The Wreck"'s Victorian biography has made it enigmatically an authentic piece in the esthetic furniture of the modern mind.

The poem's Victorian beginning of itself, of course, has not gained it its modern estimation. There are plenty of Victorian poems which are arguably just as quaint. There are deeper reasons for this poem's accepted greatness. In my mind the deepest reason is that ours is a time when the contents of the Romantic imagination still impress us as the truest response to the experience of our lives. To be sure, the original premises of the Romantic imagination, as laid down by the first English Romantics, what Coleridge called the poet's job "of spreading the tone, the atmosphere, and with it the depth and height of the ideal world around forms, incidents, and situations, of which for the common view, customs had bedimmed all the lustre, had dried up the sparkle and the dewdrops,"[1] have been modified by the intense violence of the horror-ridden human experiences recorded in the literary soul of the twentieth century. However, behind our bleeding tears lies the mythicizing gleam of expressing a new identity with life, a kind of aboriginal recovery which Northrop Frye called "a recovery of original identity."[2] Our time has been called post-Romanticism, but the prefix indicates essentially that the modern imagination is a form of Romanticism carried on into our day and has yet to be completed.

In its basic design, "The Wreck" is a Romantic poem of redemption. The poem affirms that mankind finds its identity in creative interaction with physical nature in all of its blessings and blemishes. Despite Hopkins' use of the religious redemptive myth in the old mythological images of Christianity, that is, the emblems of a free act of God offering grace to mankind as a generous act of love, he unites this traditional pattern with the new myth of Romantic gnosis, the achievement of an expanded consciousness in which the agape or love of God creates grace through an intensely personal, deeply intuitive knowledge of His redemptive love discovered in and through the world. Professor Frye called it "the power both of creation and response to creation,"[3] a description which definitely applies to "The Wreck."

Professor Elisabeth Schneider rests her fine reading of the poem on the famous Stanza 28 as expressing a genuine miracle in the old-fashioned Biblical sense.[4] Certainly this is the special moment of gnosis in the poem. However, I suggest it is the gnosis of the Romantic imaginative intellect. Hopkins depicts the "tall nun" in a kind of mystical consciousness in which she has some direct awareness of a loving Presence, a Selfhood. But more than this, given the tragic, dramatic

circumstances of this new consciousness, the nun's cry
(and Hopkins' as the religious aspirant of the first
part of the poem, reminding us that there are two great
moments of redemptive grace in the poem, though the
second is more explicit than the first) is not only a
central moment of the recognition of an original identity with God through Nature (Christ), but also it is a
cry of climactic spiritual union whose analogy to the
erotic love fulfillment of the human sex instinct is
surely a part of the poetic context. The "cry" is
more than personal identity, more than subjective love;
it is as well the generating Romantic imagination imitating the enormous powers of nature to bring forth new
words for the Word, and in that "new grace" bringing
forth a new people, a new world: a new civilization is
born. Hopkins, true to the stride of his Romantic
imaginative powers, moves from the suffering particular,
personal disasters to the triumph of a new world of
universal conversion and reconciliation. To the Romantic sensibility, between the Word of God and the poetic
word, God's revelation and the poet's, there was a cooperating creative inspiration leading to an act of
poetic-redemptive consciousness.[5] It is this grand
vision that is orchestrated in ever more resounding
sprung rhythms in the final stanzas of the ode.

One of the major reasons we revere this poem, then,
is that it is a supreme example of the Romantic imagination. The poet, indeed, has gone beyond the great his-
toric Romantics in this ode. He has dared to combine
what Professor Frye called "the two levels of nature"--
the old Classical mythology--in which there is "an up-
per world of human nature, where man was originally in-
tended to live, and a lower world of physical nature,
established as man's environment after the fall of
Adam,"[6] with the Romantic mythopoeia whereby the old
myth images are transformed into the multi-visionary
form of expanded personal consciousness.

Hopkins had the old images in his awareness coming
to the composition of his poem, but he fused them
through his imagination with the intuitive Romantic
self-consciousness. This is to say that the fall from
grace in the old tradition became a fall into questing
self-consciousness projected into time and event. History is an accumulation of our questing human self-
consciousness which gives that special plaintive ele-
giac tone to the world and works of the Romantic imagination in its uses of the past. Hopkins, in a unique
use of the Romantic vision, goes beyond nostalgia for

the old primal state, wherein there is assumed an abo-
riginally pure creation, to the affirmation of a new consciousness entering time and history in the person of
Christ (Nature) who becomes in the poem the bringer of a
new world and time. It is this union of the past and
present into a new sublime possibility which floods us
with the mystery of existence that is so attractive,
even to those who are worlds apart from Hopkins credal-
ly. Somehow this poem has become a medium to evoke a
new assent which all contemporary literature yearns
after--to quest for the hidden identity between mankind
and all existence.

* * *

For the more professional literary readers of "The
Wreck of the Deutschland," there are secondary reasons
for having the deepest admiration for the poem. First,
we are impressed with the inclusiveness of the work. It
is simply astonishing that the poem expresses a great
watershed moment in the poet's life, a national tragedy
from both a personal and private perspective, a fresh
theological view of the Incarnation, the celebration of
a miraculous inseeing insight and its providential possibilities for the spiritual destiny of England with the
ultimate implication of the reconciliation with God of
an evil, suffering world. This is a great deal to put
into any poem. The further consideration that Hopkins
was beginning to write again with this poem, after a
long period of inactivity, makes its comprehensiveness
all the more amazing.

Then there is the issue of poetic form. Modern
critics have been very impressed with the technical
problems of poetry solved in any poem, and when the poet
matches his constructive imagination against complex
structure and solves the riddle of poetic principle,
critics give great praise to such accomplishments. It
is no wonder that "The Wreck" is such a critic's delight. Hopkins in this poem experimented with his new
"sprung rhythm" and invented a new stanza whose complexity is equal to any in English poetry. There are no
tried norms for such great poetic creations, and, therefore, they remain norms unto themselves. Even those
readers who see the success of poetic form of the ode as
less than total know that they are in the difficult area
of knowing a "classic," a most treacherous critical effort.

Surely one of the most important aspects of "The
Wreck" is the structuring of its multifarious thought
patterns. Hopkins in his two-part structure has managed

to put movements, in a musical sense, in the ode, and in doing so, has found a symmetry which is organic in its unifying qualities yet balanced in its matching of a simple design with a wealth of detail filling out the design: the framing prayer pattern, opening and closing the ode, and the microcosmic personal intensity of Part I, modeling with anticipatory fineness the larger, more universal themes of Part II, are both bound in the middle by some of the most powerful narrative stanzas whose objective qualities counterbalance the great subjective, spiritual stanzas. The impression of the poem, once its thought elements have been found out, is that its poetic structure is a taut complexity, intricate in its texturing of some of the most expressive poetic diction ever used with its ebb and flow of music and meter through rich recurring images. Perhaps nowhere in all of Hopkins' writing is his idea of "inscape" more definitively exhibited.

In her widely acclaimed study of Hopkins' poetry, Professor Schneider has pointed out two criteria which make Hopkins' ode notable to modern critics. One is the use of imagery for purposes of structure. The other is the "persona" inherent in the ode. The first criterion she finds abounding in "The Wreck," but regarding the second, "the poem, like nearly all of the mature work of Hopkins will be found most unmodern and most 'Romantic.'"[7] There is no question that the personal emotional toning of the poem is almost too intense; it is also true that the reader feels in the poem, as in nearly all of Hopkins' writing, the tension of passionate verbal power about to break loose beyond all bounds and, at the same time, there is notable a counterpoise of an absolute irremissible control. These two potent energies about to collide at any instant are constantly reconciled in a fusion of opposites. Hopkins talked about the explosive character of poetry. Perhaps his own is the best example of what he meant: of course, it does not blow apart, rather it blows together. It is in this ascendance of poetic control through which the "persona" of the poem is established and ultimately dominates. The personal voice becomes the poetic voice thereby raising the statement of the poem to the level of a universal poetic rhetoric, the disembodied voice of the oracular imagination. Indeed, the poetic rhetoric of Hopkins' "persona" in all of his writing is unique among both Romantic and Victorian writers, for no other poet of that century quite managed to create that quality of public address, sumptuous in diction, elevated in style, yet having that characteristic of being addressed, spoken to, engaged, as in Hopkins' writing, especially the poetry and particularly his great ode. With so many of the great Romantics and Victorians, the reader seems to be overhearing the whispers of a private world or the conversation of an intimate scene; even pieces given a public face have a quality of the parlor or a personal meeting on a street corner about them. This is to say that public utterances by artists of the nineteenth century have a rhetorical reticence about them. Hopkins, however, charges the air with full oracular tenacity, assaulting our ears with a drumming speech. He tried to revive the rhetoric of poetic speech through subtle elevations of the poetic voice so that he might achieve eloquent poetic public address. Professor Schneider discerns this unique "persona" in Hopkins: "I am not sure that I can put my finger precisely on the means by which Hopkins transcends the difficulty of the too personal.... But at his best he does transcend it, and his success must be mainly due to his remarkable mastery over a distinguished form--after all, form is a kind of persona or serves the same purposes--and to the elevation of style, which lifts the speaker above the level of the human Gerard Hopkins to that of a universalized poet-prophet speaking as if out of a vision even when he speaks in personal terms."[8] There is an essential difference regarding the mastery of poetic form between Hopkins and his contemporaries-- the inlaying of exhibitive textures within subjective esthetic expression so that the total effect is that of a voice beyond the horizons of ordinary existence. Private intensity has become public declamation without the loss of felt personal experience. Ordinary speech has become oracular through a kind of esthetic elevation created by the mysterious fusions of imaginative intelligence. While unable to explain its origins, readers know its effects, for the greatest poets have possessed this expressive capacity. Hopkins' persona, even to those contemporary readers who find his poetic contents uninteresting, is felt and heard as a voice in our time.

* * *

Moving beyond such technical appreciations, modern critics, along with other sophisticated readers, see something more to "The Wreck." They see a handling of human experience beyond ordinary discrimination. They perceive an ultimate destiny on the horizon of this world's history. To be sure, this perception is duly enriched by the blending of intense personal experience with public eventuality, and in this union there is appreciated the creative symbolization of the expanding

70

consciousness with all of its pre-conceptual mysteries.
What is affirmed is the framing of values to contain
private experience and connect public happening. Most
of all, there is a sense of ascendancy felt in the
transformation of the subjective vision into a world-
view because there is implied the transposition of human
values from the validity of the lived, felt experience
to the great span of historical coordinators--the poet
secreted in Wales and the nun in the wreck are revealed
as having connections of an ultimate nature. It is
the thronging evocation in the ode of the personalist
vision which reaches to a higher order and purpose while
accepting this world in all of its developmental and
perfectible states--involving our personal human participation while encompassing some higher mysterious power
directing ours and the world's destiny--which we hear
as comforting music in our souls. Is it embarrassing to
say that in such poetry we hear and think and feel love?
Do we not understand down deep, in all of our recal-
citrant individuality, a call to be ourselves, as St.
Augustine expressed the essence of love, "I wish you to
be?" In the end I believe that "The Wreck" has that
taking esthetic charisma of great love poetry--the celebration of self in ever greater unions with creation.

Finally, then, this great ode is a love poem. After the subtle blend of Romantic, Victorian, and modern-
ist qualities it possesses have swirled through our
minds, justifying our celebration of it today as one of
the great odes of the English language, the lasting,
undying impression we feel is that it is a poem of heal-
ing love. Every reader, whatever his religious life,
feels this force in the poem. This chord sounds over
and over again from the first to the last stanzas. No
reader rings out these soaring swells of magnificent
poetry without believing or hoping that it is all true--
"To the Father through the features of men's faces."

Although most of Hopkins' poetry is comprised of
poems of religious love, this poem, his longest and
greatest, contains the fullest expression of what he
meant by love. Central to Hopkins' theology, religious
experience and religious psychology is the principle of
love. It was out of love that God created the world:
"God! giver of breadth and bread;/World's strand, sway
of the sea;/Lord of living and dead;..." The mystery
of the Trinity is the dark glass of creation which is
a continuing act of love in which God expresses himself
in his second person, Christ, who is the model on which
all nature and mankind were made and whose perfection

all creation aspires to imitate. Christ is the poem of
the world and all things rhyme in him. In his later
spiritual writings, Hopkins wrote little on this obscure notion of love within the Trinity, but he made
clear that deep within the shadows of the Godhead there
was laid in the fullness of divine love the creation of
the world as an expression of God's glory and that glory
would be uttered through sacrifice.[9] It was out of this
glorious love that God, the Son, took on a human nature
and came down among mankind. This supreme act Hopkins
called "the great sacrifice," as we know, a marvelous
act of joyous and adoring love which in the providence
of things became as well an act of sorrowful reparation:
"Five! the finding and sake/And cypher of suffering
Christ./Mark, the mark is of man's make/And the word of
it Sacrificed."

However, these notions are the conceptions of the
theological mind ruminating on religious experience.
"The Wreck" was written not out of the mind but out of
the heart. It is a poem full of the eastering feelings
of young love. The poetic oaths, later to become leading ideas in the reflective maturity of a brilliant
theological mind, are here poetic oaths of love which
were binding his heart, and their powerful swearings
nearly overwhelm us. Even so, these high admirations do
not move us half so much as the sheer joy and rapture
of being in love as only the young in heart can be. It
is such a falling in love with God which the poem expresses that catches us by surprise, and our own surprise
becomes a share of his ecstasy. So it is not the doctrine, which lies behind the jubilation, which takes our
hearts; it is the poetry of love expressed in all of its
human guises. We see love as courtship: "I kiss my
hand/To the stars, lovely-asunder/Starlight, wafting him
out of it; and/Glow, glory in thunder; /Kiss my hand to
the dappled-with-damson west...." We see love as passion: "Over again I feel thy finger and find thee" and
"The swoon of a heart that the sweep and the hurl of
thee trod/Hard down with a horror of height: /And the
midriff astrain with leaning of, laced with fire of
stress." We see love as submission: "Thou mastering me/
God" and "I did say yes/O at lightning and lashed
rod..."; also "I whirled out wings that spell/And fled
with a fling of the heart to the heart of the Host" as
well as "I am soft sift/In an hourglass--at the wall/
Fast, but mined with a motion, a drift, And it crowds
and it combs to the fall...." We see even the ecstasy
of love as spiritual and physical union in some passages, for Hopkins did not keep the agape of his soul

unnaturally apart from the fleshwords of his heart:
"feel thy finger," "midriff astrain," "kiss my hand,"
"hearts are flushed," "mouthed to fleshburst, /Gush!
flush the man, the being with it..." and "with fire in
him forge thy will...." This is the language of love
in the full tide of passion; these are the images of a
lover celebrating his desires for union and fulfillment
with his loved one in the swell of feeling and at the
height of desires.

So deep and so pervasive are this lover's feelings
that he did not, indeed probably could not, shunt off
the erotic undertones of his love. Human beings must
love as they are, flesh and spirit. Readers of Hopkins, chastened by the powerful integrity of his spirituality, often overlook the sexual passion in his poetry. And nowhere is this element more in evidence than
in this, his first great poem. The very physical postures through which he describes his love experiences
are sexual postures. His handling of the Passion implicit in the Incarnation of Christ has sexual undertones which become nearly surfaced in Stanza 8 in which
the poet's sense of union with Christ is expressed in
strong physical terms which evoke sexual union and consummation. Perhaps the most direct, indeed startling,
use of imagery which recalls the ever-present analogy
between religious and sexual love occurs in the notable
stanza about the tall nun calling to Christ. Exiled
because of their religious love, all of the nuns are
pilgrims of love. The tall, "lioness" nun, their symbolic representative in the poem, is not a woman
shrouded in an inhuman state of religious suppression;
rather, in terms of her human capacities, she is a total
woman in love, feeling her love for God in the fullness
of humanity as should be the case in a healthy religious
state. It might be argued that this statement lacks
evidence in that Hopkins tells us nothing about her
personally. However, taking the axiom that the measure
of a person is truly taken by one's actions under
stress, the nun's depiction was clearly meant to be
heroic. In the midst of a long, terrible, freezing-
drowning death, she kept hold of her deep commitments,
her purposed consciousness and her emotional attachments. As a nun, she had entered into a wedding of
religious love with Christ which her tragic circumstances in the shipwreck made all the more awful. In
Stanza 18, the poet, seeing her as another Mary in her
assenting heart, yet having the passionate depths of
a Magdalene, speaks of her in terms appropriate to a
great love-goddess overpowering his heart: "Ah, touched

in your bower of bone, /Are you! turned for an exquisite smart, /Have you! make words break from me here
all alone, /Do you!--mother of being in me, heart." The
poet is nearly overtaken by the beauty and passion he
imagines her love to have. Her calls are love calls,
and as she cries out her love amid the tumult of storm
and death, she is transformed into a kind of archetypal
Christian goddess whose passionate depths reach out to
all love as deep and endangered as hers from the beginning of the world. In his poetic consideration of the
nuns, Hopkins recapitulates in their heroine the many
tongues of love: "Why tears! is it? tears; such a
melting, a madrigal start!"--the many-parted passions of
love consciousness; "Sister, a sister calling/A master,
her master..."--the courtship of love; "...he scores it
in scarlet himself on his own bespoken...."--culminating
three stanzas (nos. 20-22) of love's submission, in this
case, ultimate surrender. However, the highest moment
of all is that one in which the tall nun is imagined to
experience her lover's presence. In Stanza 24 the poet
suggested that her call to Christ was more than, "Save
me!" Her call was, "'O Christ, Christ, come quickly.'"
The author wondered out loud, "What can it be, this
glee?" He imagined her as a deep-hearted woman in love:
"Is it love in her of the being as her lover had been?"
Can her love be depicted as the great love of a heroic
martyr? "Or is it that she cried for the crown then,/
The keener to come at the comfort for feeling the com-
bating keen?" He saw her, perhaps, as a saint of love
seeking "The treasure never eyesight got, nor was ever
guessed what for the hearing?" He felt her yearning for
an eternal fulfillment beyond "Time's tasking...." He
envisions her as all of these, of course, yet none explains the heights and depths of her love. The only
fulfillment for such a super passion was a supernal
lover. When she senses his coming, when she becomes
conscious of his presence to take her love, the poet is
lost for words. But those he found describe them in
the guise of two of the world's great lovers meeting, a
union in which courtship has led to acceptance, passion
to submission, assent to union: "*Ipse*, the only one,
Christ, King, Head: /He was to cure the extremity where
he had cast her; /Do, deal, lord it with living and
dead; /Let him ride, her pride, in his triumph, despatch
and have done with his doom there." Hopkins, his imagination flooded with his own love of God, here poetically
transfuses the feelings of the nuns in the shipwreck;
his triumphant fulfillment becomes theirs in the poem.
And just as was the case in his own religious love-
consciousness, the language he uses to suggest the

religious love of the nuns expresses the full range of human ecstasy--spiritual, affective, and physical.

In the stanzas following, he continues to portray this love in its fullest context of religious "fertility." In Stanzas 29-31, he portrays this spiritual engendering. Her "Wording" not only sparks all such past sublime assents, beginning with the Virgin Mary, into active memorial celebration of this new fulfilled love ("What was the feast followed the night/Thou hadst glory of this nun?"), but also engenders in the consummation of her love for Jesus, the poet imaginatively supposes, the seeds of love and eventual fulfillment (salvation) among all of her poor shipwrecked companions. These spiritual conceptions are expressed as analogies to the fruit of natural love unions. The last stanzas of the poem, then, are incantations of love, carolings to God-Christ, "Our passion-plungèd giant risen" to vaunt his love upon the world again and again until each of us finds our monumental love in him: "Now burn, new born to the world...."

The tall nun's "Wording" was more than a renewal of all such past sublime assents of plighted religious devotion, the male archetype for which was Jesus' assenting to his Incarnation and the female archetype for which was Mary's consent to be his mother in the mythology of Christianity; the potency of such love, the poet imagines, may well have engendered a new-born love of God in her poor, shipwrecked companions, thereby bringing them the fruits of salvation: "...lovely-felicitous Providence/Finger of a tender of, O of a feathery delicacy, the breast of the/Maiden could obey so, be a bell to, ring of it, and/Startle the poor sheep back! is the shipwrack then a harvest, does tempest carry the grain for thee?" These poetic sentiments are expressed in the language of the earth and the flesh, and though the poet is talking about the spiritual counterparts to consummated love on the natural level, the poetry is the poetry of human love. In all of these passionate passages, the poet captures the very psychophysical immediacy of natural love. To those who see this expression of religious passion in human terms alien to true religious love, a profanation of the spirit, the poet affirms the flesh in his love song of the soul. His justification, if he needs one, is the whole of the scriptural tradition of Christianity. He shows us in words as graphic as direct experience itself that to love with one's whole mind and heart is a magnificent activity of the entire human person.

The last stanzas of the poem celebrate Christ as
the king of God's love for creation. The overwhelming
power of divinity takes on the passion of a universal
lover who in mighty tenderness touches the hearts of
his lovers. Hopkins devotes three stanzas to exhibiting
the absolute power of the Godhead transformed through
Christ to the compelling soft touches of a personal
lover: while Stanza 32 affirms God's supreme sovereignty
"throned behind Death," Stanza 33 traces that supernatural power transformed by Christ into the merciful
whisperings of sweet love for the ears of the lover,
especially those yearning hearts almost in the despair
of their desires. Christ comes like a great knight full
of splendid affection, to fetch us from the tower: "Our
passion-plungèd giant risen, /The Christ of the Father
compassionate...." Stanza 34 hymns the great transformation of ultimate power into ultimate passion. This
is the stanza of love's consummation. Love in its
burning zeal finds, and must ever find, its mate, and
when such a union takes place, just as in natural love,
the waters of supernatural life are released in the
glorious ecstasy of communion. Hopkins beautifully exhibited the miraculous change from eternal power to
eternal passion in God through his use of the imagery of
water. In Stanza 32, water (creation) is "mastered" by
the divine power of the Creator, as the "...recurb and
the recovery of the gulf's sides, /The girth of it and
the wharf of it and the wall...." The passage exudes
supreme power and hidden control, and though the poet
tells us to "Grasp God," he seems beyond the reach of
our being. However, in Stanza 33 God's love becomes
accessible in the person of Christ who comes with "...
a mercy that outrides/The all of water...," that is,
infinite power is mysteriously superceded by infinite
love. We have a divine consolation amid the vastness
of creation (the ocean's flood) in which we drown, for
Christ is our rescuer who "...with a love glides/Lower
than death and the dark"; but he often comes in the form
of a mighty conquering power which makes his mercy, however wanted and needed, frightening and diminishing--
"The Christ of the Father compassionate, fetched in the
storm of his strides." Supernal love, while salvific,
still seems an overpowering rather than a winning of
our hearts: the "flood" of the Father has become the
"storm" of the Son. This chasm between love and power
is what makes the Incarnation so astonishing as the poet
asserts in Stanza 34: God has taken on a human nature
and now will love us as ourselves. Still divine in his
being, and thus "royal" in his nature, now he encounters
us, "Not a dooms-day dazzle in his coming nor dark as

he came..."; that is, in the Incarnation divine power
through Jesus has become divine love in human form, now
"Kind, but royally reclaiming his own...." The "flood"
of supreme power manifesting itself in the "storms" of
creation in the past now reveals itself in the "tears"
of tender forgiveness. Jesus' love lights the world
("Now burn, new born to the world, /Doubled-naturèd name
....", and in his gentle passion drowning floods and destructive storms become "...not a lightning of fire
hard-hurled," but "A released shower, let flash to the
shire," the waters of tenderness and love generating in
the fructifying graces of the communion of new life--
salvation. The poet has poetically expressed the triumphant progress of the Incarnation and the process of
Christian salvation in his making the stormy waters of
power into the sweet rain of love.

It must be remembered that Hopkins eventually saw
two great paths of God's grace. One was the consciousness of the presence of God in the inscapes of inanimate
nature, as much of his poetry reveals, and the other the
working out of that shaping design in the individual
lives of men. These strains, the one creative, which is
the context of the first part of the poem, and the other
one redemptive, which is the substance of the second
part, are the two basic themes of "The Wreck." Thus
this first great ode is all the more remarkable because
its thematic richness contained the germs of most of
Hopkins' later thinking as well as much of his imaginative engagement with the life of the spirit. However,
these two paths to God and salvation are traveled by
pilgrims of love. Hopkins preferred, as do all believing Christians I would suppose, that personal destiny be
"a lingering-out sweet skill," rather than "as once at a
crash," but the poet insists that Jesus' soft love will
buoy our hearts in this world and anchor them in the
next. With beautiful poetic appropriateness, Hopkins,
in the last stanza of the poem, brings the meanings of
his water imagery to their full implications. The
drowned nuns represent a new conception and birth
through Jesus' inseminating love of the child of saving
faith. Hopkins eulogizes the drowned nuns in the person
of their "prophetess" as the new saints of love, Christian Nereids all, who now light the path of God's love
in this world: "Remember us in the roads, the heaven-
haven of the reward...." Quite properly, the last lines
of the stanza take on a kind of Wagnerian quality, an
incantation to the King of love, a lucious-sounding
warble of love sounds, a litany of love's signs and
sighs, most of all an affirmation of love: I love you,
I love you, I love you!

This ode, then, is a great love poem. Like all great love poetry, what moves us, what takes us, is the poem's celebration of the procession of adoring love. In the first part, it is the poet standing in the furnace of his heart aflame like a Romeo beneath Juliet's balcony. Hearing him exult and feeling him rejoice in his new love of God reminds us of the tenderness and sweetness of young love. Who would not desire to fall in love again for the first time? In the second part, we are surprised at the expansiveness of his feeling, how in his love's depth he can see the poor nuns and the terrible wreck as a love-drama, how he can feel with the tall nun standing in the freezing storm and calling out to her lover to come to rescue her for himself. For Hopkins, here was the Christian meaning of Creation, the Incarnation and the Eucharist; it was "the great sacrifice" in its triumphant progress to the end of time. This choosing was an act of love like his own, and in her heart and his was heard love's oldest and sweetest song. Young Hopkins, already in love, caught the inscape of the tall nun as the beauty of a new "virgin birth," and by it he came to know a new beauty of the Lord. Her loving act in his imagination put beauty in religion and certitude in art so that he felt free to write poetry about his love of God. This is Hopkins at his best and most balanced, at his most beautiful and bountiful, "passion-plungèd" in his love for God.

In the end, "The Wreck of the Deutschland" is Gerard Manley Hopkins' new rendition of the Christian song of songs filling the air we breathe with grace and beauty. The poem is full of the language of the dearness, warmth, and sweetness of a lover. Its imagery abounds with the sighs and sights of love. Its rhythms are the love strokes of love's suitors. To read it is to hear love's whispers, to feel love's tenderness, and to experience love's promise. Whatever becomes of Christianity, however much the Christian contents of the poem have or will become a barrier to the appreciation of this poem, it remains available to every reader who can hear and feel the carol of a young heart beating with that shining new ecstasy of having fallen deeply in love for the first time.

NOTES

1. S. T. Coleridge, *Biographia Literaria*, ed. J. Shawcross (London: Oxford University Press, 1970; reprint of 1954), I, 59.

2. Northrop Frye, *A Study of English Romanticism* (New York: Random House, 1969), p. 18.

3. *Ibid.*, p. 20.

4. Elisabeth W. Schneider, *The Dragon in the Gate: Studies in the Poetry of Gerard Manley Hopkins* (Berkeley: University of California Press, 1968), pp. 26-32.

5. Frye, p. 23.

6. *Ibid.*, pp. 24-27.

7. Schneider, p. 38.

8. *Ibid.*, p. 39.

9. *Sermons*, p. 110.

BEATIFIC LANDSCAPES IN HOPKINS

It has become commonplace in Victorian scholarship today to assert that an aspect of the secularization of the nineteenth century was feeling that God had disappeared. Some scholars see this abandonment as central to Victorian religion. Literary scholars[1] frequently analyze the literary culture of the nineteenth century in terms of a religious crisis over the abscondance of God. Much of the century's literature they read as expressing the disappearance of God and a grappling for a new meaning in life by finding some substitute for religion. The new meaning was ultimately humanism in the secular city. As one scholar, J. Hillis Miller, has put it in one of the best of these studies, "The city is the literal representation of the progressive humanization of the world. And where is there room for God in the city?"[2] Secular humanism has gradually become the value system by which to explain the meaning of human life without any reference to God. In the nineteenth century, however, there was a power struggle between the forces of traditional Christianity, which still affirmed those values and symbols by which human history was seen as participating in Divinity, and those secular forces which were asserting that secular history, science, and culture had replaced God.

God's vanishment not only provides an explanation of the general culture of the age; it also explains the dominating feature of the artistic element of the culture, that is, Romanticism. The Romantics are seen as attempting to reestablish God in the universe by trying to find a new religious consciousness containing original mediating symbols between the God affirmed in a new hope in the subjective consciousness and the God witnessed anew in the objective world: "The artist is the man who goes out into the empty space between man and God and takes the enormous risk of attempting to create in that vacancy a new fabric of connections between man and divine power."[3] English Romanticism, then, was involved in trying to integrate again the shattered images of the modern landscape into a new deific vision.

This interpretation does provide one way to understand the English nineteenth century as many good scholars like Professor Miller exhibit. However, I should like to suggest, even in this age of scientific humanism, that the old viewpoint of sacral providential

history does provide an understanding of the culture of
the nineteenth century. Sacralism offers a better reading of some of the major writers of the period, especially those writers for whom religion was the major
subject matter. Indeed, I submit that it is necessary
to consider a religious view of history and human experience in discussing the religious phase of any era because insofar as religion is an authentic factor in any
culture, the corroborating sacral perspective of that
religious consciousness which provides a providential
sense of time and event is an intrinsic element of that
cultural consciousness. It will not do for historians
to discuss religious culture without any empathizing
grasp of the sacred mentality implicit in the phenomena
they are discussing. The same would be true of literary
historians. To discuss Romanticism as a major religious
movement in the nineteenth century is to seek necessarily the sacral perspectives in Romanticism. My quar-
rel with writers like Professor Miller is that Romanticism is discussed as a religious culture in which God
disappears;[4] to start with the assumption that sacral
history is inane is precisely the opposite of the basic
belief in Romantic religious culture. To begin where
the Romantics began is to affirm nature and history as
sacred and therefore to discuss Romanticism as the way
God appears to the Romantic consciousness. Scholars
like Dr. Miller attest to the fact that the Romantics
believed in God. This being so, they found God's absence in the lived quality of their culture intolerable,
and therefore called on all their creative powers to
assert that He is and lives in the hearts of mankind
and ought to reign as the best of life that is to be.
The best understanding of Romanticism, then, is as a new
articulation of the way God appears in the modern world.

    Before demonstrating the saliency of this critical
attitude by a reading of a major Christian religious
poet of that age, G. M. Hopkins, let us recall some perspectives of sacralism as expressed in Christian religious history. There have been two streams of religious
experience in Christianity. One is the theological tradition, the development of Christian thought, and the
other is the religious tradition, the record of personal
Christian experience which is the seedbed of all theology. Representing the first tradition would be figures like St. Paul, St. Augustine, and St. Thomas
Aquinas, who are among the grandest instances of a long
list of theological saints; that is, persons who have
built from a very rich personal experience of the Christian faith an elaborate rational preface for their

testimony. The direction of these stellar Christian
witnesses had always been to fuse their deep, complex
spiritual experience with a conceptual system which
would stand rational critique. It should be noted, however, that in each of these great theologian-saints, it
is unmistakably clear that their "wording" of their
experienced belief was always partial, fallible, and a
negative attempt to grasp for meaning beyond the meaning of personal assent. The other stream of Christian
history, of course, is represented by the long roster
of Christian saints (declared and undeclared), beginning
with the Apostles, early disciples and coming down
through the ages, those many saints who, in living their
Christian belief, have left records and memorials to
testify to the depth of their faith and the richness of
their religious love. It is in the record of their
lives that the Christian religion derives its vitality,
growth, and development. The source of these two
streams of Christian life, of course, was its founder,
for the name of Jesus stands for the inner witness of
personal belief ("the way"), and the name of Christ
stands for the religious intellect ("the truth"). The
two together sum up the heritage of Jesus Christ ("the
life").

Any examination of Christian history reveals that
there has been little evenness in the development of
Christian thought and belief. Some epochs seem to have
emphasized one more than the other, while there are few
in which there is a fusion of the best of each. Historians have not been very successful in explaining why
St. Paul occurs among the Apostles, a St. John among
the Evangelists, a St. Augustine among the theologians,
and so on. I would hazard a guess that the emphasis in
each case was partly the result of the need to respond
to an over-development of one tradition in the religious milieu by a counter-development of the other to
try to maintain a fruitful balance between faith and
reason. St. John may have been the result of a long
development of a stream of personal religious witnesses
of the earlier Evangelists, or a St. Thomas a response
to an over-development of medieval monasticism. Certainly it is arguable whether there has been, since
Jesus Christ Himself, a balanced fusion of the experience of religious belief and its rational conceptualization. Perhaps it has been the imbalance which has
produced the saints and heretics of the Christian calen-
dar. Out of these kinds of historical religious di-
lemmas come new champions of either "the way" or "the
truth" in an effort to synthesize "the life."

St. Ignatius Loyola can be understood in this context.[5] In a time of theological confusion in the Christian Church, he emerged a champion of personal witness as *total* dedication to the service of Christ. The society he founded upon this religious ideal became a mainstay in the Counter-reformation. As is the case with some of the greatest spiritual leaders, St. Ignatius left for posterity his own recording of his profound personal experience of the Christian faith, his *Spiritual Exercises*, a notable part of a long line of spiritual and mystical writings. What distinguished his experience was his unique method of intensifying the inner awareness of Christian witness. He sought this because he affirmed that the ground of all religion is God immanent in the consciousness. His *Spiritual Exercises* were designed to use the human faculties to render the greatest possible realization of Jesus reincarnated through faith in the very being of the believer. It is this way, he showed, that God appears in the living. There is in the Ignatian tradition a difference from earlier writers in the mystical tradition, even from those who inspired his own conversion. The difference lies in a kind of psycho-immersion into the self to find Jesus abiding and then the plunging of that Jesus-self into the world of natural being to see the transcendent Christ. There is, therefore, an Ignatian sensuousness in the *Spiritual Exercises* in the way Ignatius makes use of the senses in religious experience. The stress on the "I-witness" in belief leads to a felt insight, a felt awareness, of Jesus present and personified in the believer. This gives an esthetic dimension to personal faith which no other religious writer I am aware of provides in quite the same way. Jesus apprehended through an intensified awareness as an alter-ego to the believer produces a way to look at life and nature which reveals a special sacral quality to all existence. To Ignatius, and to those who followed his spiritual method of "I-witness" religious experience, God appears, is felt, and "plays in ten thousand places...."[6]

It is in such a sacral context, I believe, that the critic must read a Christian poet like Hopkins writing in the last century. This is so because the nineteenth century was a religious period in which there emerged a powerful counterpoise to institutionalized religion and to dogmatic theology. That counterpoise was the uniqueness of private religious assent which was how God appeared to believers in this time.[7] To study the nineteenth century Christian poet, we must examine how

his age "saw" God to locate his poetic religious vision
as we must examine his writing to discover his especial
religious consciousness in which he has told of God's
presence. In making such a study, it is useful to
borrow one of John Ruskin's most frequently used critical terms, *landscapes*, by which he meant that matrix
of images artists use to express their paradisal or de-
monic dreams of human life. These archetypal depictions
in the visual and literary arts, Ruskin believed, revealed the moral and religious vision of any historical
era; they also provided the philosophical and critical
grounds upon which to examine the quality of its esthetic
culture. In his own criticism, Ruskin described the
pattern of classical, medieval, Renaissance, and modern
landscapes. His description of the landscapes of the
nineteenth century[8] are justly famous, and to us today
prophetic, because they anticipate our sense of blight
of the earth at the time when the industrial despoiling
was just beginning as well as the vertigo of a culture
falling into despondency and ennui. Ruskin, unlike
many of his contemporaries, saw the "cloudiness" of his
age (we would say "smog"); he saw in the enthusiasm for
liberty the eccentricities of license and "the love of
wildness to ruin." He saw his age as plainly in the
umber of secularism. The landscapes of his time expressed to him a bleak profane temper, a black landscape full of dark indignant doubt about the meaning of
life. However, it would be a mistake to understand that
Ruskin, or for that matter most other contemporary
thinkers, readily accepted the umber secularism of their
time; rather many sought to find the residue of faith in
their doubts and therefore looked for beatific signs in
their culture. For example, Ruskin's great exegesis of
Turner's painting is a marvelous critique of deific
landscapes in one of the great painters of the age. The
search for beatitude in the landscape of a culture is
to begin within sacred history; it is to examine esthetic
expression for its spiritual meaning. It is to in-
quire how God appeared in the imaginative life of the
times.

   Ruskin was lamenting the absence in the deep consciousness of his artist-contemporaries of esthetic
expressions of God's spiritual transcendency, and he
could not accept their artistic expressions of religious
experience as fully authentic because of this failure
of the religious imagination. He was a true Romantic
in that he affirmed the attempts of the Romantics to
make a new expression of an original continuous landscape of God, nature, and man. This was so even though

he became profoundly dissatisfied with his own personal
religious upbringing, and he frequently expressed his
experience of God in full-blown Romantic modes of doubt,
misery, defiance, and weeping anxiousness, all aspects
of the Romanticism he severely chastised. Although he
was a true Romantic in his time, he thought he was a
Romantic with a difference. That difference was that
he started with a supernatural sense of history, experience, and faith--in a word, a strong sense of God immanent within his own consciousness. He saw the Romantic writers trying to express religious awareness within secularism, as attempting "fillers," as Professor
Miller put it, for the void left by the disappearance
of God, whereas he wanted expressions of how God entered
time and history, through personal belief and experience.

Professor Miller sees the Romantics as adventurers
and their "adventures might be defined as so many
heroic attempts to recover immanence in a world of
transcendence."[9] Their creative exploits might be described in these romance terms. However, like Ruskin,
I see their quest as attempting to recover transcendence
in their rich world of immanence and more often than
not failing to do so. In the religious phase of English
Romanticism God appears in the wondrous reaches of the
individual consciousness. The beatific landscape of
this Romanticism is a powerful interior sense of the
personal presence of God. Romantics tended to abandon
the old object-subject categories of cognition for revealing something religiously vital in the very process
of self-experience. I share Dr. Miller's sense of
romance in English Romanticism, but viewed in the context of providential history, the direction of these
writers seems just the opposite of Miller's analysis.
Their grand attempts to use the religious imagination
were efforts to recover an artistically objectified
transcendence of divine order in the universe out of
their deeply felt awareness of God in their esthetic
self-consciousness of a super-presence in themselves
and in all things. In this view, English Romanticism,
especially in its religious phase, is basically an
imaginative process of the esthetic implications of
religious immanence so that what constitutes poetic
reality is an amalgam of a special awareness in experience. This is what makes, for example, Wordsworth's
"Tintern Abbey" different as a nature poem, for in it
the poet does not imaginatively personify nature; rather
the poem is a reflective act of the poet recreating the
process of perception. This kind of use of the

imagination is phenomenological in that the central
imaginative act is the recreation of the act of personality, but in that recreation there is a recovery of a
transcendent world beyond it. The poetry produced by
this kind of creativity fuses the subject and object
thereby blurring their cognitive categorical meanings;
the imagery of this poetry is linked by way of a free
association which elicits emotional qualities that arise
from the very process of an imagined self-awareness.
The persona of the poet is multi-voiced, producing a
play of voices ranging widely and freely in kaleido-
scopic paralogical patterns imitating the movements of
the experiencing self. The landscape of such poetry,
while essentially psychological rather than cognitive,
encompasses, or tries to, the objective or transcendent
world by transforming it into the design of the self-
awareness, the immanent experience of the self. Dr.
Miller is right; there is a romance in the poetic art
of the Romantics in their attempt to harmonize and unify
human experience into a cosmic continuum through the
incandescence of the imagined self-awareness. It is at
these artistic moments that the poetic landscape strives
to become a beatific landscape, for there is in these
moments of unified being a sense of a super-presence who
is in and above all things: "And I have felt/A presence
that disturbs me with the joy/of elevated thoughts."

* * * * *

Had Ruskin known of Hopkins' early poetry when he
wrote Volume III of *Modern Painters*, he might have in-
cluded an allusion to him, perhaps associating him with
Tennyson, but making him a high-church rather than a
low-church weeper. The comparison would have been a
fair one, for Hopkins' early writing is full of orna-
mented tears; yet like all youthful poems of great
poets, they are founding promises of greater creations.
I see two themes in Hopkins' early poetry, the process
of death in natural beauty and a discontinuity between
personal faith and poetry.

The entropic process in the natural order of things
is the meaning of the Highgate prize poem, "The Escorial," "...a massy pile above the waste... Since which
no more/Eighth wonder of the earth, in size, in store/
And art and beauty" (*Poems*, pp. 3, 7). Time and event
seem oblivious to piety or royalty. "A Vision of Mermaids" (pp. 8-11) is a match piece for "The Escorial."
The mermaids sing "An antique chaunt and in an unknown
tongue." Their strain "Slumber'd at last in one sweet,
deep, heart-broken close" and disappeared forever.

Beauty cannot be kept. This pervasive sense of finitude
is the subject of "Winter with the Gulf Stream," "Spring
and Death" (pp. 12-14), "For a Picture of St. Dorothea"
(pp. 19-20), "The Alchemist in the City" (pp. 24-26),
and "The Nightingale" (pp. 29-31). There is expressed
in these poems an undeveloped abundance in the being of
natural things, an intuitive awareness that somehow
nature is deprived of a fullness which seems its due.
The sadness in these poems is that this ontological evil
cannot be made up by love or beauty, desire or choice.
The world is not its own salvation, and man cannot be
the World's savior: "Into the flat blue mist the sun/
Drops out and all our day is done."

Turning to Hopkins' early religious poetry, we
find poetic expressions of reverence and piety. We do
not discover in the writing any poetic bridge between
a deep personal experience of God and a connection to a
transcendent God throned in all existence. The artist-
believer cannot fuse personal faith and the Word in an
original wording. These poems in their attempt to express religious experience really tell us more about the
states of piety which predispose to fuller, more authentic acts of religion. As such these writings stay on
the surface of religious experience rather than recording the underside depth of religious consciousness.
They are representations of the manners of religion,
but this public decorum of reverence and piety may be
discontinuous with an abiding, richly profuse experience
of personal faith in all of its secret and private ema-
nations. As a recitation of public prayers, they seem
at times more engaged with language than experience,
but they were for Hopkins poetic experiences in which
he explored the figurations of words, their rhyming
capacities, and the subtleties of lyric movements.

These general remarks apply, for example, to "Barn-
floor and Winepress" (pp. 16-17), which is an attempt
to express the sacrifice of Christ in the conventional
Biblical symbols of nature--harvesting wheat or grapes.
The poem is an exercise in the management of words. The
same is true of "New Readings" (p. 18), though here in
Hopkins' attempt to write a Biblical poem, there is a
conscious imitation of George Herbert. Again Hopkins
is concerned for framing language, plotting symbol,
conveying pattern as is the case in nearly all of these
early poems, not unsurprisingly since they are exercises. However, they are more than this, at least some
of them are attempts to reach beneath manner, beyond
composition to personal meaning. "Where art thou

friend..." (p. 22), for example, dares hint of a filial
relationship, perhaps, with Digby Dolbin, that is bound
up in a religious crisis. "The Alchemist in the City"
(p. 24) reveals a secret self hidden within the public
show: "The whole world passes; I stand by." In "Myself
unholy" (p. 26) the poet tried to tell about personal
pollution as the beginning of alienation, but lines like
"Yields to the sultry siege of melancholy" say more about
the poet's imitative diction than his experience. If
"See how Spring opens..." (pp. 26-27) truly refers to
Hopkins' conversion to Catholicism, the poem rather
than being joyful tells us more about stylized spiritual
weariness, a kind of frozen tumbling into conviction
and a falling on the other side of the line. The same
general spiritual malaise is expressed in "Easter Communion" (pp. 20-21) and "See how Spring opens with dis-
abling cold." "My prayers must meet a brazen heaven"
(p. 27) is a portent of the last sonnets, but the "bat-
tling in the poem is less a hurling of prayers to a
fortressed deity than a "warfare" between words and
feeling in which diction seems impervious to authentic
emotion.

        Reading these early poems from the vantage point
of the great religious poetry of the mature period, I
find it significant that at this early stage of development, Hopkins seemed to have no deep, personal experience which forged and shaped his poetic powers. In
"The Half-way House" (pp. 28-29), for example, he tried
to affirm his need for experiencing a sensuous love of
God, a felt sense of Divine presence, yet the poem ends
reciting a formula to his religious tension: "...enter
these walls, one said: /He is with you in the breaking
of the bread." In "Nondum" (pp. 32-34) he again took
up his need for a developed consciousness of God within
him, for a powerful sense of Divine immanence; however,
in this instance while poeticizing patience as a conventional spiritual predisposition, his feeling broke
through unsatisfied and asserted itself in appealing
familial terms: "Speak! whisper to my watching heart/One
word--as when a mother speaks/Soft, when she sees her
infant start, /Till dimpled joy steals o'er its cheeks."
Yet these feelings are timid and meek. Religion is
still a sweet disturbance, the negative experience of
which "The Habit of Perfection" (p. 31) sings so lyri-
cally. Hopkins had yet to be plunged into a positive
encounter with God in his poetic consciousness. Somehow
the Anglican milieu was one in which he felt he had to
chase God. These early poems are expressions of religious experience which are winded and weak as God fleets

through the shadows of awareness, half-way up the moun-
tainside of the mind, beyond each day's grasp. The
poet cannot connect through his utterances his self and
nature and God. Heaven and earth cannot be worded by
the grace of the imagination. These poems show the
religious crisis to be the absence of a personal spiritual capacity to personify God in the creative consciousness. We are reminded of Wordsworth's "obstinate
questionings" and Coleridge's "beautiful and beauty-
making power." There is no crisis of belief in a
transcendent God in these poems; the crisis is finding
him immanent in feeling and thinking, actions and
words.

* * * * *

It is clear that converting to Catholicism did gal-
vanize Hopkins' personal religious consciousness. As
Professor Miller has carefully noted, Hopkins' intellectual, poetic, and religious development called for
a complete system of relationships in which nature,
beauty, and self are united in a consciousness of God.[10]
However, too much stress can be put on the doctrinal
ambiguities or lack of a complete theological system in
Evangelical Anglicanism as a disordering force in Hopkins' religious life. The muddle of Deistic ideas and
Wesleyan emotion that became the mixed nature of nine-
teenth-century Anglicanism, no doubt, created an unbalanced environment in which to settle into deep religious
awareness.[11] But by the time Hopkins was a young man
at Oxford, the Tractarian movement had profoundly
changed the religious fervor and practice of Anglicanism. And these changes should be seen in the context
of a total movement of religious thought in the century, a development which is a major aspect of English
Romanticism.

It should be recalled that the kinds of answers
being given to the basic questions about the religious
heritage of the eighteenth century were Romantic.
Coleridge, the most important English Romantic writer
on religion, took a position on the nature of faith
which became the intellectual ancestor of the Oxford
Movement. That position stressed belief as an affective
commitment generated out of the total human experience.
As Professor Basil Willey has noted, to Coleridge,
"Faith, like Imagination, is alive and creative, ever
realizing its own objects."[12] Professor Willey quite
significantly underscored "realizing its own objects,"
for it is the internal process of religious faith that
Coleridge saw as the foundation of personal religious

experience, and it is upon this foundation that theology and liturgy develop. Moreover, Professor Willey went on to show that this emphasis on religious feeling within the whole human experience (not limited to reasoned attitudes) as a springboard for religion is fully coordinate with the position of John Henry Newman in his *University Sermons* and *The Grammar of Assent*. Newman himself in his old age looked back to his Oxford years with his fellow divines as a fellow-traveler of the English Romantics such as Wordsworth and Scott.[13]

Religious historians have seen the Oxford Movement to be partly caused by the Romantic movement. From the perilous state of religious confusion at the beginning of the century, English religion had developed into a potent force in the life of Victorian England.[14] This happened partly because English thinkers got in touch with religious and intellectual currents on the continent as well as a new creative engagement in English letters with personal religious experience.[15] Professor Owen Chadwick summed up the impact of the new Romantic spirit on religion:

> Theology like literature moved from reason
> to feeling. But theology did not move be-
> cause the human spirit yearned for a new
> depth. A world of common sense yielded
> to a world which saw common sense shallow
> and reached after beauty and truth beyond
> the easy fetters of prose. Religious men
> wanted poetry of heart in their hymns,
> sacramental sensibility in their worship,
> recovery of symbolism in art and architec-
> ture. But Keble and Newman and Hurrell
> Froude were not divines of the Protestant
> right wing because they were romantics.
> They expressed their divinity with the aid
> of romantic images and attitudes common
> to their day.[16]

The effect of this religious ferment on the Church of England was profound. Though the Puseyites weakened the Church in politics and popular esteem, "they strengthened the Church of England in its soul.... No one did more to drive Anglican worshippers out of formalism, to give them a sense that Christianity has a history and a treasure not insular, and to enable sympathetic hearts to perceive the beauty and poetry of religion.... As moral guides representing in their persons the ideals of sacramental and ascetic life which

they commended, they [Newman, Pusey and Keble] sent to
the English conscience a call which sounded through the
century."[17]

Thus there is a need to correct two views of Romanticism which are regularly articulated in contemporary scholarship. One is that Romanticism, especially
in its religious phase, was Christianity without belief.[18] In its deepest and most profound implications,
the Romantic was committed to the affective base of personal religious experience, and that commitment, as I
have tried to suggest earlier in this essay, was really
an affirmation of one of the basic dynamics of the Western Christian tradition, indeed, precisely the kind of
shift in religious interest one would expect as a reaction to the rationalized theology of the eighteenth
century. Secondly, the Romantic concern for the phe-
nomenon of God as an immanent creative activity in the
life of the imagination likely represents an attempt to
articulate out of this new subjective religious spontaneity a fresh vision of Creation as a radiant and
hierarchical order--the world as God's symbolic book. A
resurrection was attempted of a new lexicon of God's
meanings (Hopkins' "instress and inscape" are just such
instances) which has always been allegorical, that is
typological, even in the direct verbalization of Revelation. This pulling together of faith and nature as
manifestations of God's presence as the Incarnated
Christ is a recovery of an old affirmation in Christianity. But it grows out of a *realized* faith in which a
new carol is made of the discovery that Christianity is
validated in human experience. Insofar as Romanticism
is an extended religious consciousness, it is an intuitive insight of God's transcendence in the world.

It is not surprising, then, that Hopkins was caught
up in this new Romantic religious zeal even if, in his
time at Oxford, the Puseyite movement was in its ebb-
tide. However, he was not primarily engaged, nor was
he ever deeply involved in the great public questions
of reaction and reform in English religious life. He
was profoundly concerned with vivifying his own personal
religious belief, with seeking his own salvation. In
this regard, Professor Miller puts heavy stress on the
Roman Catholic doctrines of the Incarnation and the
Eucharist as the linchpin of Hopkins' system, for only
in affirming the reality of God's sensible presence in
the world can poetry, belief, and God come together.
Professor Miller is undoubtedly right in this doctrinal
emphasis because Protestantism had "thinned out" the

meaning of the communion service and thereby had weakened the notion of the Incarnation. While this integrity of the Catholic theological tradition very heavily influenced Hopkins' conversion, what was settled for him were largely intellectual difficulties which bore in on his personal belief. There still remained for him to *realize* the Incarnation and the Eucharist within himself and in all things as a real presence. The assent marked by his conversion guaranteed no realization of Christ immanent in him or in unleavened bread. For centuries before and since, Catholics have assented to the doctrine of the Incarnation and the Eucharist without making that deep affective commitment to an experienced sense of the presence of God. I do not believe that Hopkins' conversion alone accounts for his life as a priest or his work as a poet. The difference between disciple and versifier and priest and poet was an internal process of election so devastating that he was radically changed forever.

Fifteen years ago I argued that the best account of Hopkins' mature writing lay in his experience of St. Ignatius' *Spiritual Exercises*. Rereading the scholarship since then and living with the poetry for twenty-five years has not changed my mind though I see new reasons for understanding the power of the Ignatian spirit on him. In my earlier book on this subject, I explicated Hopkins' understanding of the *Exercises* and went on to exhibit that understanding as permeating his writing. However, the design of that study was mainly methodological, the juxtaposition of the Ignatian meditative method with the basic poetic patterns. I uncovered in the intellectual springs of the poems the ricochets out of the Ignatian spiritual process.[19] I now want to suggest a supplementary reading by stressing the religious psychology of the poems.

* * * * *

The difference between the early and the mature religious poems is that God appears in the latter and is only talked about in the former. By "appear" I mean that the poet has experienced a Presence in his inner consciousness which he has verbalized into an expressive form. The nature of this inner awareness is a participation by some supreme Presence in the very substance of the personality. The experience of this amounts to a realization at an affective level of what is meant by the Incarnation. I mean by "affective realization" that there takes place in the voluntary intelligence a pattern of felt awarenesses which generates a sense of

93

a powerful, loving Person present whose self-being is
at once perceived as beyond the limits of human nature.
To use Hopkins' own words,[20] "For human nature, being
more highly pitched, selved, and distinctive than anything in the world, can have been developed, evolved,
condensed, from the vastness of the world not anyhow
or by the working of common powers but only by one of
finer or higher pitch and determination than itself and
certainly than any that elsewhere we see...." It is
significant that this awareness grows out of self-
awareness, "...when I consider my self-being, my consciousness and feeling of myself, that taste of myself,
of I and *me* above and in all things...." Hopkins in
his opening commentary on *The Spiritual Exercises* has
expressed the touchstone of his Ignatian Spirituality.
To develop a love of God as a living faith, the spiritual exercitant must first develop an appreciation of
himself as an "unspeakable stress of pitch, distinctiveness, and selving, this self-being of my own." It
is the plunge into self that reveals the Incarnation:
"We may learn that all things are created by consideration of the world without or of ourselves the world
within. The former is the consideration usually dwelt
on but the latter takes on the mind more hold." This
is to say that proofs of God's existence as First or
Last Cause of all things are the usual ways philosopher-
theologians try to invoke a sense of Divine transcendence. But the consideration of "the world within"
ourselves is by far a more powerful means of realizing
God participating in creation through the Incarnate
Christ.

While it is true that *The Spiritual Exercises* read
like a series of general guidelines for meditating,
they are really a rich psycho-meditative process for
energizing religious awareness.[21] The history of their
development and practice stresses their psycho-religious dynamics in bringing the exercitant to a religious love so powerful that the self is shifted "...to
a higher, that is better pitch of itself; that is to
a pitch or determination of itself on the side of
Good."[22] The basic pattern of this development is a
deep encounter with the self in order "to see" within
what I shall call "beatific landscapes" in the psycho-
geography of the personality. This involves encounter-
ing the self in deep reflective acts through the exercise of external and internal awarenesses so that there
is created a felt self-discovery:[23] "I find myself with
my pleasure--and pains, my powers and my experiences,
my deserts and guilt, my shame and sense of beauty, my

dangers, hopes, fears, and all my fate, more important
to myself than anything I see." It is important to see
in the discovery of "self-being" a justifiable pride of
being: "But to me there is no resemblance: searching
nature I taste *self* but at one tankard, that of my own
being." It is in "this throng and stack of being" that
God is realized. Out of a sense of goodness comes
awareness of a greater goodness. Human nature is at
the top of the scale of being, and in contemplating
what this means as an expression of second person of
the Blessed Trinity as a creating participant in all
things, is to realize "that God is deeply present to
everything...that it would be impossible for him but
for his infinity not to be identified with them...."
The beatific landscapes of religious consciousness reveal nature and persons as charged with God's being in
the personal presence of Jesus unifying in love all
creation. The energy of this triunity is love because
this personal Presence appears in esthetic qualities
whose sensible beauty appeals to the voluntary intelligence and beckons to the arbitrary intelligence. Hopkins affirmed Duns Scotus' rational psychology because
he posited the will and intellect as the complex of the
rational nature of man with the will the superior
force.[24] This was how Hopkins understood his experiences: love, not knowledge, is the supreme force in
man's nature and thus to love is a free act in response
to the lovable, in the case of God, the supremely
lovable. The apprehension of God in Christ under the
appearance of the beautiful, that is, in theological
terms, grace, lifts the consciousness towards its fulfillment. Grace is God's beautiful appearance in the
consciousness revealing a glimpse of the infinite unity
of all being in Christ's Presence and thereby carrying
consciousness to a higher level of creation. This understanding of the Incarnation overflowing the consciousness was Hopkins' way of practicing *The Spiritual
Exercises*. This was how he understood the psycho-
religious techniques in the *Exercises* of seeing, feeling, touching, and tasting the Gospels in order to
realize Christ's presence in the self. This is, as
St. Ignatius put it, the "foundation" upon which all
elected love depends. But faith does not happen without personal encounter and transformation. As Hopkins
wrote in his *Commentary* on the *Exercises* of Ignatius'
"Contemplation for Obtaining Love," "All things therefore are charged with love, are charged with God and
if we know how to touch them give off sparks and take
fire, yield drops, ring and tell of him." It is the
knowing "how to touch them" that is at the heart of the

Ignatian spirit. With this kind of religious knowledge, the landscapes of personal consciousness reveal
a Divine Presence and thus are transformed into beatific
landscapes full of the spirit, life and joy of God.
This is my understanding of Hopkins' grasp of Ignatius'
religious psychology.[25]

* * * * *

When Hopkins wrote "The Wreck of the Deutschland,"
the echo of a new rhythm "which was haunting" his ear
was more than a new prosody. It was more than his conversion to Catholicism which in itself did not account
for the beatific landscapes he was experiencing. The
poetic impulse of this work derives its power from a
new, intense, transforming, touching ("stressing") of
self and things through which Hopkins came to an overwhelming realization of God participating in his being.
Out of this "instressing" there was made visible to him
a whole range of beatific landscapes. This terrifying
and awesome awareness of the priest finds its expression
in the poet as "a new rhythm," a new riming in Christ.
I quite agree with Professor Miller that this felt
realization in the priest became an "ultimate guarantee
for the validity of metaphor"[26] in the poet, for through
his intense experience of sharing the very being of
Divinity through the Incarnate Christ makes all things,
all persons, and all events "news of God." However,
this understanding of creation as the drama of God
develops out of the psycho-drama of the world within
ourselves. A new realization of immanence leads to a
new recollection of transcendence.

These fresh beatific landscapes are the very substance of Part the First of the "Wreck." The poet
celebrated that out of his serious contemplation of the
distinctiveness of his self, he had apprehended an intimation of God in his being. The consequences of this
filling realization were overpowering, for God's
mastery of everything was truly made manifest to him.
It is significant that Hopkins expressed this realization as a "wreck." The violence of the Ignatian religious psychology expressed as physical violence in the
poems has a basis in the *Spiritual Exercises*, as I have
pointed out, indeed, might have had a basis in Hopkins'
own experiences of the *Exercises*.[27] I have come to
believe now that Hopkins has to some extent dramatized
the religious happening in the first part of the poem to
balance the drama of the shipwreck in the second part.
This makes artistic sense because the psycho-drama of

religious experience, being more a happening than an
event in the consciousness, needs an external typography
to record its occurrence. The imagery of the beatific
landscape of the first part of the poem is made up of
physical counterparts to psycho-religious states. The
great achievement of this part of the poem was in the
poet's ability to find appropriate concrete images to
convey the passion and the power of religious realization, the movement from the discovery of the masterhood
of God through terror and majesty, violence and love.
No religious poem in the English language manages the
wording of these personal experiences of beatific landscapes more effectively.

The second part of the poem is an "objective cor-
relative" for the first part. Hopkins had found a new
transcendental sense in his own surcharged religious
consciousness. He was able to "touch" a catastrophe
like a shipwreck and "see" beatific landscapes allied
to his own "winter and a warm." Though Hopkins did
describe the wreck objectively, this part is really
about his new-found ability to extend his full religious
consciousness beyond himself. This was the new excite-
ment of both his religious and poetic powers. The focus of his extension, of course, was the tall nun, the
"lioness," the "prophetess," the "virginal tongue told."
It is from Stanza 18 on that the poem begins to become
an expression of multiple religious consciousness--his
own fictionalized in the first part and typologized in
the second. The poet's very intense realization of his
religious sensibilities, the main matter of the first
part, provided an extended visionary meaning to an
otherwise absurd tragedy. Thus the poet imagined the
nun as possessing his own vivid sense of God's presence
within her, and because of the powerful religious awareness the poet imagines for her, she is able to confront
bravely the "babble" of the disasters, able to be lifted
above "the tumult" because she possessed a new beatific
landscape of higher meaning which braced her thoughts,
words, and deeds. All of the religious powers attributed to the nun were really those of the poet who was
inscaping "the unshapeable shock" night. The tall nun
was the foil for Hopkins' new faith.

Hopkins left no doubt about the ambivalences of
the multiple religious consciousness which had entered
the poem. In Stanza 18, he wondered whether she shared
in her religious experience something like his own
Ignatian transformation. Was she "touched" like him?
Did it hurt the same way? For inspiration in this riddle of faith, he appealed for a helping poetic grace to

97

assert his inscaping of her. In the fullness of his
own religious sensations, he was moved to share her
tears, but the whole cast of his awareness was to wonder about her spiritual experience in terms of his own.
This divided sensibility is overcome in Stanza 19, for
the poet affirmed a unified or continuous faith between
himself and the nun: "Sister, a sister calling/A master,
her master and mine!--" The common nature in faith of
all belief is Christ. Now the poet was able justifia-
bly to intermingle the objective description of the
nuns (Stanza 20: "She was first of a five..." and Stanza
21: "Loathed for a love men knew in them...") with his
new-found faith, for theirs was a unified religious
sensibility. They had a common meaning in Christ.

The priest in his faith was re-enacting sacral
history. He believed in the unity of religious consciousness between himself, the nuns, and Jesus. In
Stanza 22 he expressed this coherence in the mystical
coherence of the Passion: "Five! the finding and sake/
And cipher of suffering Christ." This same figuration
ricochets into Stanza 23 which is about the stigma of
St. Francis, to whose religious tradition the nuns be-
longed. The poet was quite aware of his construction
of a poetic religious identity between the nuns and
himself as is clear in Stanza 24 where he described his
own secure surroundings: "I was under a roof here, I
was at rest,..." And though he narrated the tall nun's
call on Christ from the newspaper account he had read,
in Stanza 25 he again wondered what was in her consciousness: "The majesty! what did she mean?" The entire stanza is one of trying to validate a multiple
religious consciousness which he poetically has fused.
In his rumination, the poet further explored the connections within sacral history searching for a typological meaning between the nun's plight and the near
shipwreck of the Apostles on Lake Gennesareth. The
poet's words attempted an identity of religious experience, a unifying typology via sacred history, yet the
best connection that can be made in poetry was metaphorical. The degree to which art and poetry can be
validating inscapes of the Presence of God in the un-
folding sacred history of religious consciousness is
at best problematic, that is allegorical.

Stanza 26 continues the wonderment of the poet's
felt identity with the nun's in the wreck. Of course,
in exploring their spiritual realizations, he was exploring his own. The poet asked whether it was a para-
disiacal vision which was the source of their intense

realization of God's Presence: "...the jay-blue heaven appearing/Of pied and peeled May!" In Stanza 27 he asked whether it was weariness of life which pitched them to higher levels of awareness: "No, but it was not these./ The jading and jar of the cart, /Time's tasking, ..." He judged it was more like this than the immediate dangers of the storm because such pressures allowed no time to develop one's religious consciousness, no time to meditate the Passion as he had had in his own quiet, safe-harbored tempest. The stanza ends in a kind of poetic bafflement as to what moved the nuns, especially the tall nun, to seem to have the same intense realization of God appearing on the horizons of the soul.

Coming to Stanza 28, which is the center of the second half of the poem, Hopkins tried to express the omnipresence of Christ as dramatically entering the tall nun's religious consciousness. Indeed, it might be argued that this stanza is the center of the entire poem, for in part one, Hopkins did not attempt to directly express the Presence to whom he said "Yes." However, in this passage, he tried to find words for the felt participation of God in the consciousness. Unlike the secular historian who searches for outside causes and internal motives, the poet of sacred history tries to grasp the para-logical religious forces which work in and through the human awareness, forces which seem to have a shape and direction of their own in an overpowering, commanding way. But all the recorder can do is represent these powers. In Professor Miller's idea of English Romanticism, Hopkins was the arch-Romantic here because he seemed really to have been trying to find original symbols of a new sense of God in the consciousness, in nature, in time, and in the world.[28] The question is whether poetry can adequately express the religious consciousness of self, nature, and Christ.

I submit that the Romantics proved that poetic art cannot. This is the hubris of their dedicated and valorous attempts. Their failures define the limits of personality, art, and belief. This is no less true for Hopkins. Stanza 28 is Hopkins' affirmation of the limits of poetry. In the identity of religious consciousness he felt between Christ, himself, and the tall nun, that is, in the vivid sense of Christ's Presence in time, in nature, in himself, in the tall nun, he was as a poet at a loss for words. All he could do was dramatize his un-wordedness. Man (poet) cannot word

99

God's Presence directly. Religion is not art, but religious art can speak of the psychology of religious
experience. The artist can construct metaphorical
bridges between nature and God if the self is the thea-
ter of the religious drama where the affective experience of God present can be glimpsed and thereby represented in the context of the whole human soul. Stanza
28, then, was the poet's "touching" of his own belief
experiences as they expressed his own feelings of the
nuns and the wreck as metaphors for his own beatific
landscapes. He was wording the wreck out of his own
religious sensibility. Any perceived union between the
inscapes of self, nature, and God that man makes is
subjective, limited, and problematical. Insofar as
Creation is a proportional representation of the Creator, so any reflection of Deity is by way of a negative
analogy. Religious poetry is locked into the experiencing consciousness. That is the significant element
in the religious phase of Romanticism. These writers
rediscovered the original source of religion itself,
the believing consciousness. What bellows through the
"Wreck," is a new poetic awareness born of a fresh and
unique religious psychology, a new intensification of
an affective consciousness of God. When Hopkins heard
about the tragedy, he took it in with his new-found
Ignatian realization, and he poetically bridged their
"wreck" with his own. By doing so, he found original
words for celebrating his own beatific landscapes in
their tragedy. The last orchestrated stanzas of the
poem are really the virginal telling of his own lion-
like prophecies about the ways he "saw" God working in
the world. The mysteries lay in his faith of which the
poem is the ritual.

In sacral history, the flux of all things in time
feels the stress of the mystery of the Incarnation:
"But it rides time like riding a river,"[29] a mystery
which is realized in the believing consciousness in and
through and by which the Incarnation is perpetuated.
Such was Hopkins' concept of the priest, and the priest-
poet attributed this conception to the nuns, particularly the tall nun: "Word, that heard and kept thee
and uttered thee outright." But was this attribution
the poet's vanity? Poetry, Hopkins had affirmed in his
aesthetic credo, could inscape the poet inscaping nature. Natural landscapes, however, become beatific
landscapes only by virtue of the experience of faith.
It is this mystery of realization that validates the
metaphors of religious poetry as beatific landscapes of
Christ: "Since, tho' he is under the world's splendour

and wonder, /His mystery must be instressed, stressed; /For I greet him the days I meet him, and bless when I understand." Though belief in the Incarnation is based upon Christ omnipresent in Creation, this insight of faith must be realized in the assenting consciousness to the point of an intimation of Jesus' living presence in the very soul, an encounter which is full of spiritual joy and vision.

This mystery instressed validates through faith, self, and nature. In poem after poem after the "Wreck," Hopkins celebrated the spiritual joy and vision of his realization. But in every case, the religious drama is not Christ present in the world; it is Christ apprehended (instressed, stressed) as present in the world. Thus it is not poetry that is the prime vehicle for beatific landscapes; it is the religious awareness. It is spiritual exercises which vivify the mystery. Each of Hopkins' mature nature poems is in part or whole a dramatization of religious consciousness in action, lifting the mystery, sifting the mystery of the Incarnation in ever grander joyous vision. In nearly every poem, there is an Ignatian emphasis on deepening the religious awareness through vivid, concrete instances of the flash of the Divine Immanence in things breaking out in the creating consciousness. This affective realization (desire-love) grows to an overwhelming attraction to elect to serve (assent-choice) the Sovereign of the soul. It is love that moves the soul to commitment. The ground and growth of love are so strong in Ignatian Christianity, as Hopkins understood it, that he, perhaps in the force of that love, over-stressed the division between choice and desire in human nature, a division which became sharper and personally unbalancing in the deep religious experiences in his later life and work.

From "God's Grandeur" to "(The Soldier),"[30] Hopkins found aesthetic symbols for his subjective religious consciousness. Flushed with spiritual intimations of Jesus in his life, he "saw" Christ as King of the Universe, just as Ignatius expected from anyone who truly entered into his *Spiritual Exercises* with a full and generous heart. In his excellent account of Hopkins' "system," Professor Miller constructed a theory that Hopkins developed a system of words, of self, and of nature, but could not find any unifying principle until he appropriated the Catholic doctrine of the Incarnation.[31] In his own understanding of this doctrine, Hopkins was able to affirm a principle of existence

common to words, self, nature, and God. I agree that
Hopkins searched brilliantly for a unified understanding of the basic elements of a philosophy of language,
psychology, science, and religion, but he failed to
bring them together. Unlike Dr. Miller, I see the mature poems as instances of this failure. As passionate
and powerful as they are as metaphors of Hopkins' rich,
religious consciousness, they are self-expressions,
self-assertions, a dazzling mosaic of inscapes of self.
Their power comes from a fusion of the inscapes of words
with the inscapes of self. Language was structured by
transforming imagination into a design of the self, for
poetic language is a distinct and original revelation
of self. However, this liberating of self into art is
also a vaunting of self because poetry is the utterance
of a new creation, what Hopkins called a new "sake" or
design not yet created. This coincides with what
Coleridge said, that poetry is "...a repetition in the
finite mind of the eternal act of creation in the infinite I am."[32] While literary art is a sublime participation as an act of creation, it is also self-serving.
Before Hopkins was very far into developing his "system," he realized this implication. So profound was
his growing understanding of this, he was brought to
burn his youthful poems when he became a Catholic and
entered the Society of Jesus. Even religious poetry inspired by a new intensity of loving God perceived in
his soul had the creative design of self stamped on the
utterances: "But MEN OF GENIUS ARE SAID TO CREATE, a
painting, a poem, a tale, a tune, a policy; not indeed
the colours, and the canvas, not the words or notes,
but the design, the character, the air, the plan. How
then?--from themselves, from their own minds."[33] Indeed, Hopkins' understanding of the notion of art, its
creation and its role in culture was in fact a consideration of a heroic deed done to beautiful individua-
tion. So while the poet, the finite creator, can bring
together words for himself (Hopkins' early poetry would
be an instance) and words for himself selving nature
(his mature poetry), nevertheless his own personality
is the original, singular, individual "arch-especial
...a spirit" of the literary art. The creative imagination understood this way presents an insurmountable
moral impasse to serving God utterly and completely.
Hopkins had a deep initial awareness of this which is
why he burned his poetry in the first place and why he
never saw fit to accept the writing of more poetry
afterwards as suitable for a true man of God. These
creations were proud participations in the creative
grace of the Incarnation, not humble correspondences

102

through religious works. Consequently I would differ with Professor Miller: while Hopkins' new-found realization of the Incarnation in Ignatian Catholicism may have brought together his theories of the inscape of words, self, and nature into some tentative intellectual alliance, his deepened awareness of the character of full religious charity in the context of his own grand constructions, in fact, heightened the barriers for him between religion and art, priest and poet. He understood, as only the father of his poems could, how easy it was to succumb to admiring the design of the creator rather than the mark of the Creator. I suggest that the history of his writing proves how right he was. Saying this, to be sure, offends the secular mind and grieves the pious aesthetes: "(And here the faithful waver, the faithless fable and miss)." But to Hopkins the Incarnation meant giving up his poetry in the name of serving Christ present in his assenting consciousness; moreover, the fact that he did write poetry was a blot on his Christian service record, a serious one. He had no responsibility for becoming a poet in the world; his duty was to love and serve God with his whole heart and soul and mind. This explains the burning of this distress at the beginning and the terrors of his last confessions. What he did permit himself to write had to be written with a vigilant indifference as to its destiny. So unlike Professor Miller,[34] I read these remarks in a late letter: "Feeling, love in particular, is the great moving power and spring of verse and the only person that I am in love with seldom, especially now, stirs my heart sensibly and when he does I cannot always 'make capital' of it, it would be a sacrilege to do so,"[35] as meaning more than religious consciousness was the inspirational power of his poetic creativity, though it was; I think it means that the deepest acts of religious experience are not fit for constructing into proud inscapes however beautifully designed, even those special sensible awarenesses which are conducive to artistic creation. The father of grace and the father of poetry are not the same no matter how he wished it might be so.

Herein lies the key to reading Hopkins' last poems. Why were these writings so astringent, spare, and judgmental compared to the mature poetry of the middle period? The answer is, I believe, that Hopkins had reached that stage of his spiritual development under the tutelage of *The Spiritual Exercises* where he had to face up to Ignatius' own counsel about the proper use of things: the Christian use of all things must lead back to God through the imitation of Christ. This

meant finding in one's life a spiritual counterpoise to
Jesus' "Great Sacrifice," as Hopkins called it. Hopkins
began increasingly to realize that for him this meant
giving up his poetic ambitions. Of course this one
part of his life was supremely desirable, and thus denying this character in himself was as close as he could
get to Christ humbling His Divinity by becoming man.
Hopkins knew this to be the ultimate test for his spiritual life, especially since his priestly ministry
seemed so unproductive. Moreover, he seemed to sense
in his ill health that his life was coming to an end.
Death and judgment occur frequently in his last writings; his election of Christ was all the more vital and
necessary.[36]

This spiritual movement from a sensuous religious
love to an elective religious love is at the heart of
the Ignatian spirit. Hopkins understood this spiritual
ascent in Ignatian spirituality from the first retreat
onwards and all of his subsequent writing is a record
of his own religious journey to reach an Ignatian state
of charity. "We lash with the best or worst/Word last,"
he wrote in the "Wreck." *Lash* suggests striking in a
desperate, difficult reaching out; it also suggests
carefully tying oneself to a safe anchor to prevent being lost in the violence of the death storm. "God's
Grandeur" laments the failure of mankind to connect to
God through the grandeur of His creation. "The Star-
light Night" explicitly urges the buying and biding of
"Prayer, patience, alms, vows" to purchase a new consciousness of "Christ home, Christ and his mother and
all his hallows." This call to "--Have, get, before it
cloy, /Before it cloud, Christ, lord..." is one major
theme of exhortation which threads all the mature
poetry. It comes from the religious urgency of Hopkins'
Ignatian spirituality.

The other major theme, as most readers know, is
the failure to discover in human experience the higher
consciousness of the Incarnation and therefore descending into the oblivion of "...man's last dust, drain fast
towards man's first slime." To ascend to the viewpoint
of Creation through choosing Christ involved no rejection of nature or mankind: "Man's spirit will be flesh-
bound when found at best/But uncumberèd...." Without
Christ instressed, Hopkins believed that human beings
see their undoing all around them: "It is the blight
man was born for, /It is Margaret you mourn for." Perhaps Hopkins' grimmest statement of not electing the
vision of the Incarnation was in his poem "Spelt from
Sibyl's Leaves" in which he dramatically envisioned

104

man's natural destiny of coming to an absolute end unless he chose the saving grace of belief in Christ. The
poem makes powerfully clear that the choosing involves
emulating the "Great Sacrifice" of Jesus, that is, en-
acting in one's life total love even to death. Hopkins
knew what a transformation of spirit this involved, that
it took great moral courage. In this poem he expressed
in mental and physical terms the reality of Christian
election in the self "Where, selfwrung, selfstrung,
sheathe- and shelterless,¦ thoughts against thoughts in
groans grind." There is a personal passion in loving
Jesus, another sacrifice.

        Thus from the beginning and throughout his reli-
gious and poetic careers, Hopkins was intensely aware
of the tough implications of being a full Ignatian disciple of Christ. For him, even more than for many fellow Jesuits who did or do not possess his profound
spirituality, his vocation meant going beyond his own
stamping of glimpses of Christ in his poems. It meant,
like Jesus Himself, not choosing to assert his lofty
powers of self-assertion as a poet, to give spiritual
beauty back by not making artistic beauty. Of all the
interpretations of his famous sonnet, "The Windhover,"
I think this is the best one. While the chivalrous bird
enacts the power and the glory of God in his magnificent
execution of his created nature (and whoever sees him
and all nature through him could not but be stirred to
marvel at his achievement and mastery), yet it is even
a greater, more heroic deed done in God to subdue the
creative self. For to have full power and to elect not
to display it in action out of the higher intention of
denying your self-creating valor was to imitate in hu-
mility the "Great Sacrifice" of Christ's heroism. Hopkins understood the Incarnation as essentially an act
of love expressed in the monumental act of Christ's re-
signing His infinite Godhead for the finite nature of
man. This Self-denying act "graced" human life, that
is, raised human life to a new spiritual consciousness
and thus a new existential destiny. So if Christians
"Buckled" on Jesus' great spiritual nature as the bird
had his created nature "buckled" to Christ's created
nature, then "Brute beauty and valour and act" becomes
"the fire that breaks from thee then, a billion/Times
told lovelier, more dangerous, O my chevalier!" Hopkins here managed a powerfully expressive metaphor of
Christ in created nature and the realization of Christ
in human nature. Without denying the news of God in
the bird, he affirmed the sublime utterance of the Word
in religious love.

There is, however, a major personal irony in this attitude. The inscaping of the bird acting out himself and the inscaping of the priest acting out himself are the result of the self-inscaping of the poet seeing and saying it all. The utterance is the poet's and therefore the poet's act, like the bird's, is a proud "striding/High there," from which that "billion/Times told lovelier" *fire* does not break. As Hopkins lived his vocation and struggled with his poetic desires, he came to realize this Christian paradox ever so deeply.

The spiritual awareness underlying this poem, and others like it, is that Creation is finite, which in Christian understanding means that nature is deprived of a durational fulfillment. Therefore its beauties, while providing beatific landscapes, move through generational cycles indifferent to the fate of any individual beauty. This ontological evil in nature encompasses man insofar as he is a natural creature. He too is swept into "Million-fueled,¹ nature's bonfire...." Thus the majestic enactment of the windhover reveals a beatific landscape, to be sure, but a passing one, for chance and change will obliterate wind and wing. So the hidden poet, however enthralled, must transcend the acts of nature (his and the bird's) by a higher act of human willpower, born of a spiritual consciousness, if he is not to be a midge on a little journey from womb to tomb. For while in Christian consciousness, the Incarnation permeates all of Creation as its source and exemplar, especially emphasized in Ignatian spirituality, yet Christ as the second person of the Holy Trinity calls for a supernatural faith. Such a faith is a vow of love which is honored in the choosing to humble oneself by sacrificing one's gifts in the service of loving God and man as oneself, if ascendance out of the cyclic fire of nature is to be attained. Through this charity one is elevated to become another Christ whose promise was salvation. This act of self-immolation is the result of what Professor Miller quite accurately called "the terror of grace," that mysterious process of Divine providence in which God chooses the victim in His creative grace, the very act of the purifying sacrifice itself through His mortifying grace and finally the ascendance to God in the grace of elevation.³⁷ In this context "The Windhover" proclaims the mystery of these graces lying in the believing consciousness, explaining the events of existence beyond history.

While Hopkins' unique individualization of Christianity has full and firm ground in the history of the

Christian experience, readers have tended to see his
emphases as shaped by Victorian and Protestant rather
than Roman Catholic traditions. While it did so appear
to me at one time, I now am convinced that this explanation will not do because it leads to misunderstanding
the last poems as mysticism, which I do not believe
they are, or as heterodox, which they certainly are not.
If Hopkins' life and writings are searched for a con-
tinuity of religious experience within the Christian
tradition, there emerges a clear pattern. He began
with a strong religious instinct (his early writings),
cultivated his religious awareness to a point of deep
spiritual consciousness (his mature poems and spiritual
writings) and then in the fullness of his development,
he tried to reach in his personal and spiritual life
the full implications of his charity--every thought,
word, and deed dedicated to Jesus, the Son of God. He,
of course, understood that in the concrete living of
his belief in the Incarnation, his human nature in its
sense and emotional interlocking with the natural world
seemed extricably bound to the merry-go-round in the
finite world. Such was all the more dangerous to his
religious spirit, for in his continual visions of beatific landscapes in natural experience, which he celebrated in the rich spontaneity of his poetic personality, he was lured to accept a natural destiny. Still
from the beginning of his aesthetic and religious experiences, as his writings attest, Hopkins had a constant insight breaking in on him that the fate of nature, poetry, and personality was the same, destruction.
If Christianity meant anything, it meant overcoming this
natural evil.

As the development of his religious and artistic
creativity steadily reveals, he regularly sought to
reach beyond the destiny of Creation to the resurrection of salvation. After becoming a Catholic and Jesuit, he drew on his deepened and intensified spiritual
consciousness making his own life as a priest, sometimes
poet, an ever increasing struggle to emulate Jesus.
This was his own sacrifice which, as it evolved in the
last part of his life, meant exclusively concentrating
on those experiences which furthered making his personality in Christ's image. This in fact involved
letting go, so far as possible, his human desires. In
his case, it is fair to assume that his supreme human
desire was his poetry to which he had to become indifferent if he were to live up to his vocation as he saw
it. This meant, as he called it, affirming his elective
will rather than his affective will. All genuine

believers are called to be saints. Absolute election was what was involved, as in the whole history of the Christian experience all the lives of the great saints illustrated.

Viewed in this way, Hopkins' last poems are fit expressions of the last stage of his developing religious consciousness. In his early priestly career, he could suspend the ultimate implications in his vocation of the full and complete election of Christ, for the counterpoise to his sensations and emotions celebrated in his poetry was a rich beatific landscape flooding his creative imagination. Moreover there was the promise of his priestly ministry as a counterpoise. The very rhetoric and rhythm of these poems suggest a plunging into the poetic personality realizing itself in lush, rich self-expressions of nature, God, and man. This is the poetry of the natural will rejoicing in its concurrence with nature. This is the poetry of Hopkins, the Romantic, building metaphoric bridges between his religious realizations and the outside world. But now, in his advancing spirituality, he became convinced ever so completely that personality is nature humanized and poetry personality stylized. Despite the taking vistas of beatific landscapes, these spiritual-aesthetic territories must be overlooked. Not to do so was to share their finite fate--the destruction of their world. He had to go on to the beyond of infinitude, God Himself, where his Ignatian understanding was leading him. To do so meant making that final, irrevocable, tough choice, that ultimate election to "...wish all, God's better beauty, grace."

The last poems, then, are poems of the elective will. Once I thought them to be Ignatian in an ambiguous way,[38] but I now think they are the most Ignatian poems he wrote. Their very subject matter is the religio-psychological process achieving a final and ultimate election of Christ as King of the soul. Therefore it is no wonder that these poems are taut in style, spare in diction. The language is in fact adversary because the poetic argument is basically a trial of the conscience. The poetic feeling is the trauma of self-accusation in all of its psychosomatic pain and suffering. I think it is appropriate that these poems occur after the one titled, "(The Soldier),": "Mark Christ our King. He knows war, served this soldiering through...."[39]

"(Carrion Comfort)" is Hopkins' Lucifer poem. The poet struggles to hold himself together after being

pitched from the paradise of dwelling on his own beauty
and power. Like Milton's Lucifer, the poet, having been
completely overwhelmed by the terrific force of God Al-
mighty in his consciousness, now tries to hold himself,
his selfscape, together. Psychologically, the poem is
about keeping the ensigns of sanity themselves from being hauled down. Spiritually, the poem is about the
terrible judgment of infinite power destroying the pride
of the rebel soul. The feelings are a mixture of fear-
ful punishment, abject defeat, and obstinate wonder of
survival. Lucifer, self-beauty, clings to some asser-
tion of self-existence after the tumult of spiritual
warfare, searches for the meaning of his defeat, finds
a joy in his own capacity for utter destruction. This
sonnet is Lucifer's song in Hopkins' soul: love
destroys.

This poem is a cornerstone to all of these last
poems. If Hopkins was to make that total and final
election of Christ being first and foremost in his life
(and we must remember that this was a prime concern of
his religious life as his last retreat notes make
clear),[40] then he had to suffer the complete and utter
defeat of his personal nature, that is, his sensuous
intelligence, his philosophical "system," his drawing,
his music, all that expressed his commitment to himself in the form of attachments to his own creations,
especially his poetry. The true and complete dislodge-
ment from loving his own nature with all of its gifts
of intellectual and creative powers was, to be sure,
like a fight to the death. The most significant bat-
tles are the silent ones within, and they defy logic.
Why must love be seemingly intertwined with hate?
Particularly why must Divine love destroy human charity?
The age old answer is the mystery of evil, that unfulfilled condition of being teasing us in its abundance
that it is complete and thus securing our love. The
goodness of nature and human nature appears so beautifully fulfilling to our sensuous intelligence that we
lose the spiritual insight where being falls off into
non-being, where its goodness disappears because it
ceases to be at all. This discovery of our fatal love
comes, if it comes at all, at the height of self-awareness, self-powers, self-instressing. The Lucifer of
the self, as the archetype, is high on the scale of
being; Lucifer represents treason at the top in an effort to assert his own inscape, to dwell on his own
beauty. He must betray over and over again to try to
become something more. The spiritual action of self-
pride is an intimidation from the heights of being, the

good ruining from the good, the best in us deliberately reaching down, falling into the regions of self-hatred which becomes a mad selfish dream of undoing. Only higher creation strives to storm the towers from which its real fall ensues--that strange love-hate to try to reverse creation. Lucifer's song is a love song about ruining heaven. It comes from no mean spirit in us, for hell is a work of our nature at its best.

This toppling of the towering "I" in us to the dark defeats of the brink of nonbeing is the subject of the sonnet, "No worst, there is none." This poem is the pandemonium in the pit of the hell of self. The poem is full of wrenching grief and sadness. The poet grimly states that strange and odd condition of self thrown back on itself, discovering the meaning of the defect of finitude, where the "I" breaks off into nothing at all: "...all/Life death does end and each day dies with sleep." This sonnet is Hopkins' song of the demons of self in the hell of personality.

"To seem the stranger" marks a shift in these poems from the spiritual war within to its public sur-facings. Hopkins may well have viewed his assignment to Ireland as an outward sign of his inner strife over his deep attachment to his affective nature and his priestly super-nature. The "third remove" is an in-between state brought on by a lull in the battle be-tween the spiritual and material consciousness: "dark heaven's baffling ban/Bars," and "hell's spell thwarts." So long as the battle wages within, and there is no victory, his being is "idle," reduced to the brink of nonexistence, unwording, unbeing, "a lonely began."

The sonnet, "I WAKE and feel the fell of dark, not day" is a poem about eternal damnation, his everlasting separation from God. What dominates the spiritual con-sciousness in its penetrating realization of being locked forever into the limitation of human nature is a nightmare torment of dark and endless hours of aware-ness (I wake and feel) and that one's eternity is no more than being "in solitary" with oneself. This poem is a description of spiritual imprisonment in the "tank" of self where no cries are heard or heeded. The soul in its ultimate solitude is helpless, left to be its own victim, hopeless because it cannot rescue itself. No poem of religious experience gives more powerful expression to the state and feeling of being cut off from the source of life, God, and His grace. Hopkins here recorded how intense his spiritual realization was

that human nature is finally no more than itself, that
selfhood is "God's most deep decree," that tasting its
self-bitterness is part of the design of purifying grace
to see that "The lost are like this...." The poem
marked the nadir of his spiritual descent in his struggle to choose Christ above everything else. It expressed Hopkins' harrowing of hell.

The poems that follow are expressions of how Hopkins thought God through His grace raised his self-
sacrificing soul to salvation. They should be read in
conjunction with his other spiritual writings revealing
how he was finally able to make his supreme election
with no holding back. Helpless and hopeless, the spirit
waits, must wait, for God to move it upwards to an
ascending level of love: "Patience, hard thing!" One
crucial spiritual battle is nearly over, but the war
with self must go on: "Yet the rebellious wills/Of us
we do bid God bend to him even so." Steady in self-
sacrifice, the subdued heart can be left to self-
patience and charity. Let be rather than rejected in
tormenting torment, in the heart "...joy [will] size/At
God knows when to God knows what...." But grace comes
from above at God's bidding, not man's, and when it
comes, "the very view of personality" is touched and
lifted "from one self to another self, which is a most
marvellous display of divine power":41 "...whose smile/
's not wrung, see you; unforeseen times rather--as
skies/Betweenpie mountains--lights a lovely mile."

In the sonnet, "My own heart let me more have pity
on," Hopkins devised some words which expressed the
dislocated elements of human nature in its fallen
state: "Soul, self; come, poor Jackself, I do advise/
You, jaded, let be...." This string of personal epi-
thets was his way of describing the divisions in the
soul between its human and spiritual nature. At God's
behest, graces come to the "affective will" as a supreme
good (to which it automatically responds) and if one's
"pitch" or "elective will" corresponds to the notice,
then the soul is brought from the psycho-spiritual
"hell" of the rift between choice and desire to the
"heaven" of a new union of the powers of the soul which,
Hopkins believed, moved man literally to a new selfhood,
a higher consciousness, a closer relation with God.
Thus the climax to the "terrible crystal" sonnets is
the sonnet "That Nature is a Heraclitean Fire and of
the comfort of the Resurrection." In this poem Hopkins
wrote in his full poetic power of his insight into the
ontological evil of Nature's fiery finitude, man's

tragic place in the turning furnace, and Christ's great heroic act of snatching him, his combustible being burned away, from the ashy oblivion of his material destiny and raising him to the Godhead Itself. Hopkins here expressed that transforming religious realization of the miracle of Christian faith. To the nonbeliever, the statement is simply impossible, words, words, words! But to the Christian poet, steeped in his belief, the chaos of life which the words represent, emblems of the disorder in the soul: "This Jack, joke, poor potsherd, patch, matchwood...," are transformed through grace to the Word: "...immortal/diamond, /Is immortal diamond." Christ became human and thus humanity became Christ. In the final awareness, out of the rage of grace comes a new self, filled and flooded with the Presence of Christ. This is mankind's way back to fulfillment in God forever.

Readers who see these last poems as expressions of an absconded God, it seems to me, have in fact turned them upside down. Putting them in the context of sacral history, which is to say, within religious consciousness and experience, these poems are marks of an advanced development of personal faith. They give hints of a deepening of Hopkins' realization of God in his life and his response to that new consciousness. God was not absent or out there somewhere, but frighteningly present in the assenting awareness of spiritual experience. To be sure, there was an intense cognizance of the transcendence of God, "The swoon of a heart that the sweep and hurl of thee trod/Hard down with a horror of height...." But if the self is so inclined, God descends into the human heart: "Father and fondler of heart thou hast wrung: /Hast thy dark descending and most art merciful then." In Hopkins' case these last poems expressed his real wreck (he had an intimation earlier when he heard of the *Deutschland* and the sisters); he was standing amid the spiritual storm of his priestly life calling to Christ to come quickly. The call was out of the deep soul because of the felt Presence of Christ there. However small is the human role in the drama of salvation, and Hopkins understood it to be very small, still there must be that act of love to actualize heavenly grace. And this act itself is dependent upon a realization of the Incarnation in the religious consciousness transforming through self-sacrifice "creative" graces to the fullness of charity. In terms of the history of Christian spiritual experience, this realization of the Incarnation in the soul is full of overwhelming awe.

I think the reason that modern readers find religious writing like that of Hopkins disconcerting is because it is usually read in basically secular terms. Thus Hopkins is read as a Romantic, humanist poet. But this would be to say that he got no further in his poetic expressions of his religious mentality than those Romantics who at best tried to find some aesthetic bridges between their own religious intimations of God as present in themselves and in the world. Without belittling these Romantics, it is not possible to talk of pure beatific landscapes in their poetry. For example, in Wordsworth, there is not evident in his development as a man and poet any significant growth of religious experience after those early, first, bright, moving hints. Personally he may have grown a great deal in his religious consciousness, but there is no illuminating record of it in his poetry. While it is fair to style Hopkins' early poetry as Romantic humanism, indeed even in some of these poems, he went beyond this Romanticism. He was impelled to grow in his religious experience in such a way that he surpassed that phase of Romanticism which is a form of humanism. For he could not abide the reduction of belief to the subjective consciousness alone without any saving connection to an outer and higher scale of reality. This resulted in a form of religio-aesthetic imprisonment, as is clear from the quasi-pious confessional cries of contemporary literature written in the Romantic tradition for the past one hundred and forty-five years. The whole spirit, direction, and culmination of Hopkins' writing was to record how God worked in his soul. This is why those qualities of spiritual destitution, which is the principal subject of humanist Romanticism, are not in Hopkins. Therefore, however powerful was his personal attachment to his poetic nature, he did not confuse the artist of God for the priest of God. He held steadfast to his belief that art was an emblem of man's finite nature, "Manshape," and like human nature, "his firedint...is in an enormous dark/Drowned." Poetry is not religion; metaphors do not lead to salvation. God can integrate Himself with nature and man; poets can interrelate nature and consciousness; but only God can amalgamate the Creator with Creation. Perhaps this is the special insight of Romantics which is the source of their agony and peculiar tragedy both real and artistic. Their hubris is that they think they are prophets of God. In going beyond humanist Romanticism, Hopkins' beatific landscapes brought him to realize profoundly that he was the servant, not the prophet, of the God in his consciousness because that God, he believed, is the Lord of Creation and the Master of the World. His religious assent meant ultimately giving up, so far as possible, his self-pride (his intellectual and artistic genius) in order to show, like Jesus, his model, that he loved purely and truly. This sacrifice of the creative ego in the human personality seems impossible to the ordinary Romantic because it is the very sign of his nature and personality. To give self up willingly would be self-destruction. Hopkins' art is a record of his sacrifice out of his love of God. Perhaps only Romantics know the wreck of that sacrifice even if few can fathom the mystery of its doing; nevertheless, they are witnesses if not prophets. As for Hopkins, his poetry became God's landscape.

NOTES

1. Joseph Hillis Miller, *The Disappearance of God: Five Nineteenth Century Writers: Thomas DeQuincey, Robert Browning, Emily Brontë, Matthew Arnold, Gerard Manley Hopkins* (Cambridge, Massachusetts: Harvard University Press, 1963) is a definitive example.

2. *Ibid.*, p. 5.

3. *Ibid.*, pp. 13-16.

4. *Ibid.*, pp. 1-2.

5. See David A. Downes, *Gerard Manley Hopkins: A Study of His Ignatian Spirit* (New York: Twayne, 1959), Ch. 2.

6. Quotations of Hopkins' poems are from *Poems of Gerard Manley Hopkins*, ed. with additional notes, a foreword on the revised text, and a new biographical and critical introduction by W. H. Gardner and N. H. MacKenzie (4th ed.; London: Oxford University Press, 1967). Hereafter *Poems*.

7. See David A. Downes, *The Temper of Victorian Belief: Studies in the Religious Novels of Pater, Kingsley and Newman* (New York: Twayne, 1972).

8. See Harold Bloom, ed., *The Literary Criticism of John Ruskin* (New York: Doubleday Anchor, 1965), pp. 77-110. For an extensive analysis of Ruskin's sacral view of art and the imagination see my *Ruskin's Landscape of Beatitude* (Ann Arbor, Michigan: University Microfilms International, 1980).

9. Miller, p. 15.

10. Miller, pp. 308-11.

11. See L. E. Elliott-Binns, *Religion in the Victorian Era* (London: Lutterworth Press, 1964), pp. 131-52.

12. Basil Willey, *Nineteenth Century Studies* (New York: Columbia, 1956), pp. 90-92.

13. *Ibid.*, pp. 92-101.

14. Elliott-Binns, Ch. 2.

15. *Ibid.*, pp. 132-34.

16. Owen Chadwick, *The Victorian Church*, Part I (London: Adam and Charles Black, 1966), p. 174.

17. *Ibid.*, pp. 230-31.

18. See M. H. Abrams, *Natural Supernaturalism: Tradition and Revelation in Romantic Literature* (New York: Norton, 1971).

19. *Ignatian Spirit*, Chs. 5 and 6.

20. *The Sermons and Devotional Writings of Gerard Manley Hopkins*, ed. Christopher Devlin (London: Oxford University Press, 1959), p. 122. Hereafter *Devotional Writings*.

21. *The Spiritual Exercises of St. Ignatius Loyola*, tr. Thomas Corbishley, S. J. (New York: P. J. Kenedy, 1963).

22. *Devotional Writings*, pp. 148, 151.

23. *Ibid.*, p. 122.

24. See *Ignatian Spirit*, pp. 44-51.

25. *Ibid.*, Ch. 4; also *Devotional Writings*, p. 195.

26. Miller, p. 313.

27. *Ignatian Spirit*, pp. 52-57.

28. Miller, pp. 13-14.

29. *Poems*, p. 53.

30. *Poems*, pp. 66-99, which encompasses virtually all of his major poems after "The Wreck" to the last sonnets.

31. Miller, pp. 311-15.

32. Samuel T. Coleridge, *Literaria Biographia*, ed. John Shawcross (London: Oxford University Press, 1907), I, 202.

33. *Devotional Writings*, p. 238.

34. Miller, pp. 317-24.

35. Claude C. Abbott, ed., *The Letters of Gerard Manley Hopkins to Robert Bridges* (London: Oxford University Press, 1955), p. 66.

36. *Ignatian Spirit*, pp. 115-30; D. A. Downes, *Victorian Portraits, Hopkins and Pater* (New York: Twayne, 1965), pp. 77-83; *Devotional Writings*, p. 129.

37. *Devotional Writings*, p. 158; Miller, pp. 346-49.

38. *Ignatian Spirit*, pp. 135-36.

39. It is interesting that these last poems of Hopkins are interspersed with poems like "Tom's Garland," "Harry Ploughman," and "St. Alphonsus Rodriguez," poems which depict the character of hidden heroism in various human predicaments—the poor unemployed, the lowly farmer, and the humble religious. Each is presented as meeting his fate with an uncommon courage, an inner splendor, and a providential destiny. Perhaps these examples of "seldom sick, /Seldomer heartsore...," "Amansstrength...," and "...the war within...the heroic breast" were metaphors for his own human struggles.

40. *Victorian Portraits*, pp. 78-83; Miller, p. 357.

41. *Devotional Writings*, p. 151.

119